EVALUATING INNOVATIONS, SAFEGUARDING SYSTEMS, & SHAPING THE FUTURE OF SECURE FINANCIAL TECHNOLOGIES IN CYBERSECURITY

Tolulope Komolafe

Evaluating Innovations, Safeguarding Systems, and Shaping the Future of Secure Financial Technologies in Cybersecurity

Published in Nigeria in 2021 by Plexity Digital

A catalogue record of this book will be available from the National Library of Nigeria.

TABLE OF CONTENTS

Preface iv
Foreword vii
Introduction x

Chapter 1
The New Security Paradigm in the Cloud Era 1
Chapter Two
Anatomy of Financial Fraud and Digital Threats 11
Chapter Three
Risk Management Frameworks and Compliance in Finance 22
Chapter Four
The Role of Artificial Intelligence in Fraud Detection 32
Chapter Five
Blockchain, Transparency, and the Future of Secure Transactions 43
Chapter Six
Building Cyber Resilience in Financial Institutions 53
Chapter Seven
The Human Factor in Financial Cybersecurity 63
Chapter Eight
Cloud Security and Financial Infrastructure 72
Chapter Nine
Data Privacy, Ethics, and Regulatory Alignment in Cybersecurity 80
Chapter Ten
The Future of Financial Cybersecurity, Innovation, Governance, and Global Resilience 88

Reviews 96
References 98

PREFACE

The story of modern finance is the story of connection. Every bank transfer, card payment, or mobile transaction represents a link in a vast global web of systems that communicate, calculate, and decide in fractions of a second. Behind these seamless experiences lies a reality that is far more fragile than most realize. A single vulnerability in a line of code, an overlooked configuration, or a deceptive email can disrupt not just an organization but entire economies. In this age, the health of the financial sector depends on more than capital and confidence. It depends on cybersecurity.

I began writing this book because I saw a growing gap between technological advancement and systemic security awareness within financial institutions. Over the years, my work in cybersecurity has shown me that finance and technology are deeply intertwined yet often speak different languages. Bankers think in terms of risk, compliance, and returns, while cybersecurity professionals think in terms of resilience, detection, and control. The intersection of these worlds is where our collective future lies and bridging that divide is the purpose of this work.

Evaluating Innovations, Safeguarding Systems, and Shaping the Future of Secure Financial Technologies in Cybersecurity is more than a technical guide. It is an invitation to rethink how we secure financial trust in a digital era that is constantly testing the boundaries of possibility. My intention is to make complex cybersecurity principles accessible to decision-makers, students, and professionals who want to understand how technology can be both a tool for growth and a gateway for risk.

The book begins by establishing the foundation of financial cybersecurity. It explores how fundamental concepts such as confidentiality, integrity, and availability extend beyond theory to form the invisible architecture of financial safety. It asks what happens when that architecture fails, and what can be done to strengthen it before the next crisis strikes. From there, we examine how threats have evolved, from crude phishing attempts to advanced persistent attacks powered by artificial intelligence. Each chapter moves from the known to the emerging, guiding readers through the ecosystem of risks that define modern financial systems.

Throughout this work, I have relied not only on research and frameworks but also on lived experience. I have seen institutions that appeared impenetrable fall victim to small oversights. I have seen teams recover from devastating breaches through cooperation, foresight, and discipline. These experiences shaped my conviction that cybersecurity is not a department or a checklist. It is a culture. It begins with leadership and extends to every employee who handles data, makes decisions, or interacts with customers.

You will find in these pages an integration of real-world case studies, including incidents that reshaped global cybersecurity awareness. Each is included not to recount failure but to extract lessons that can guide the future. Whether it is the story of a bank that lost millions through a fraudulent transaction or a fintech startup that strengthened its systems through proactive auditing, each example demonstrates how knowledge, preparedness, and collaboration can transform vulnerability into resilience.

The book also turns toward innovation. Technologies such as artificial intelligence, blockchain, and secure cloud systems are not simply tools to improve efficiency. They are instruments through which trust can be rebuilt in a digital economy that often struggles with visibility and accountability. I argue that the path forward requires a mindset that does not separate innovation from security but rather sees both as interdependent forces driving progress.

In the later chapters, I address the significance of regulation, governance, and international standards. Financial institutions today operate in a regulatory environment that is increasingly complex. Laws such as the General Data Protection Regulation (GDPR) and frameworks like the Payment Card Industry Data Security Standard (PCI DSS) exist not to restrict innovation but to reinforce responsibility. Understanding and integrating these frameworks are vital steps in creating financial systems that are both competitive and trustworthy.

While this book presents strategies, frameworks, and case studies, it is also deeply personal. Writing it allowed me to reflect on my own journey across the intersections of finance, cybersecurity, and policy. I have learned that progress in this field does not come from technology alone. It comes from awareness, integrity, and a shared commitment to protect the systems that sustain livelihoods and economies.

For professionals, I hope this book offers new perspectives on managing cyber risks in financial operations. For students, I hope it provides a clear foundation for understanding the complex dynamics of financial technology security. For leaders, I hope it emphasizes the truth that cybersecurity investment is not a cost but a safeguard of reputation, trust, and long-term growth.

We stand at a defining moment in digital finance. The future belongs to those who can innovate securely, anticipate threats intelligently, and govern responsibly. My goal in writing this book is to contribute to that future; to inspire a generation of professionals who understand that security is not an afterthought but the foundation of sustainable progress.

FOREWORD

The relationship between finance and technology has always been defined by evolution. From ledgers and checkbooks to mobile apps and blockchain, each wave of innovation has brought both progress and exposure. Today, financial institutions stand at a crossroads. The speed of innovation is extraordinary, yet so is the sophistication of threats. In this complex environment, few professionals have managed to connect innovation, regulation, and security as clearly as Tolulope Komolafe.

When I first encountered her work on cybersecurity in financial systems, what struck me most was her balance of technical understanding and strategic vision. She has a rare ability to explain the logic of algorithms and the psychology of fraudsters in the same conversation. In an industry that often divides specialists into silos, Tolulope stands out as someone who sees the full picture. She understands that protecting a financial institution requires more than advanced encryption or monitoring systems. It demands leadership, foresight, and the ability to shape culture.

This book is both timely and essential. The financial world has entered an age where data is wealth, and breaches are more damaging than market fluctuations. Regulatory bodies have responded with frameworks like the General Data Protection Regulation (GDPR) and the Payment Card Industry Data Security Standard (PCI DSS). Yet compliance alone does not guarantee safety. What Tolulope presents here is an expanded vision of cybersecurity that connects regulation with innovation. She shows that the most resilient systems are not those with the most expensive tools but those guided by clarity, accountability, and trust.

The chapters that follow explore the real meaning of financial security in a digital age. Readers will find thoughtful analyses of fraud detection mechanisms, artificial intelligence in threat monitoring, blockchain technology in financial transparency, and the complex ethics surrounding data privacy. The discussion is both global and local, with lessons drawn from international case studies as well as insights rooted in African financial systems.

Tolulope writes with the precision of an engineer and the clarity of a teacher. Her tone is practical without being overly technical, reflective without being abstract. This makes the book useful not only for cybersecurity professionals but also for financial executives, regulators, and students seeking to understand how digital trust is built and protected.

What makes this work exceptional is its focus on collaboration. Tolulope emphasizes that cybersecurity in finance is not an individual effort. It is a collective commitment that involves banks, fintech startups, technology providers, and policymakers. She reminds us that innovation can only thrive in an environment of shared responsibility. In this sense, her book is not only a manual for protection but also a manifesto for partnership.

Every institution that manages digital transactions will find value in these pages. Readers will come away with a stronger understanding of risk, a renewed respect for compliance, and a practical roadmap for embedding security into their operations. The book's greatest strength lies in its ability to humanize cybersecurity. It treats technology not as an end in itself but as a tool for building financial integrity and public confidence.

As financial technologies continue to reshape global economies, the question is no longer whether institutions will face cyber threats but how prepared they will be to withstand them. Tolulope Komolafe's work offers answers rooted in expertise, discipline, and vision. Her message is clear: true financial innovation cannot exist without security.

It is an honor to introduce this book to readers who are shaping the next chapter of finance. May it serve as both a guide and an inspiration to build systems that are not only smart but also safe.

INTRODUCTION

The digital transformation of finance has been one of the most powerful revolutions of the modern era. What began as the automation of transactions has now become an ecosystem of interconnected systems, algorithms, and platforms that move trillions of dollars every day. Banks, fintech startups, and payment processors are no longer simply custodians of money. They are custodians of data, trust, and identity. Yet, this progress comes with complexity and risk. As technology expands the boundaries of what finance can achieve, it also multiplies the number of ways it can be attacked.

In this new financial reality, cybersecurity has emerged as the cornerstone of confidence. No innovation in banking or investment can succeed without trust, and trust depends on security. Every data breach, every fraudulent transaction, every system failure is a reminder that financial technology is only as strong as its defenses. The speed of digital transformation has outpaced the speed of regulation, and in that gap, vulnerabilities have flourished.

This book was written to address that gap. It is built around one central idea: **the protection of financial systems must evolve alongside innovation**. Technology has changed not only how money moves but also how crime operates. Fraudsters, hackers, and organized criminal networks now use advanced tools to exploit the smallest weaknesses. From deepfake voice frauds to AI-powered phishing campaigns, the threats have become more adaptive and less predictable. The financial sector can no longer rely on traditional firewalls or compliance checklists. It must adopt new forms of intelligence and governance that anticipate rather than react.

The chapters ahead will explore how financial cybersecurity has evolved from a technical concern into a global priority. Chapter One examines the foundations of security in finance, explaining the principles of confidentiality, integrity, and availability that underpin every secure system. Chapter Two investigates the anatomy of fraud, showing how malicious actors exploit human and technical flaws. Chapter Three dives into compliance and regulation, explaining why adherence to frameworks like GDPR and PCI DSS is more than legal formality. It is the basis of operational resilience.

Artificial intelligence and machine learning take center stage in Chapter Four, where we analyze how predictive analytics can detect fraud before it occurs. Chapter Five introduces blockchain technology and its promise of transparency and immutability in financial transactions. The following chapters explore secure cloud architectures, case studies from real-world financial breaches, and frameworks for building resilience into institutions. Finally, Chapter Ten looks forward to the future, exploring how technologies such as quantum computing and zero-trust models will redefine the security landscape.

The objective of this book is not to overwhelm readers with technical detail but to present a structured, realistic approach to safeguarding digital finance. Each chapter blends research with practical experience. You will find examples drawn from global institutions, emerging markets, and startups across Africa, Asia, and Europe. The lessons are universal, grounded in the understanding that while the tools of finance may differ, the principles of security remain constant.

In writing this book, I wanted to create a guide that speaks to several audiences at once. For cybersecurity professionals, it offers updated frameworks and emerging strategies for defending financial systems. For business leaders, it provides insights into integrating cybersecurity into corporate governance and strategic decision-making. For graduate students, it offers a comprehensive foundation for understanding how financial cybersecurity operates in practice. And for policymakers, it highlights the importance of cross-sector collaboration in shaping safer digital economies.

The most important thread running through this work is the idea of **resilience**. No system, however advanced, is completely immune to attack. What defines a strong institution is not the absence of incidents but the capacity to respond, recover, and rebuild. Financial cybersecurity today is as much about human preparation as it is about technical sophistication. Teams that train regularly, communicate clearly, and build a culture of vigilance are better equipped to face emerging threats than those relying solely on automation.

Another core idea explored in this book is the balance between innovation and regulation. Financial institutions must continuously innovate to remain competitive, but they must also operate within regulatory boundaries that protect the integrity of the system. Innovation without accountability creates fragility. Regulation without adaptability creates stagnation. The solution lies in the middle ground: a governance model that allows creativity to thrive while maintaining rigorous oversight.

Throughout these chapters, I have emphasized that cybersecurity is not an end state but an ongoing process. It is dynamic, responsive, and evolutionary. The threat landscape changes daily, but so do the opportunities to build stronger defenses. By combining artificial intelligence, blockchain, encryption, and human intelligence, the financial sector can achieve a level of protection that is not just reactive but predictive.

At its heart, cybersecurity in finance is about people. It is about protecting the millions of individuals who trust their banks, payment platforms, and investment firms with their most valuable information. It is about safeguarding livelihoods, reputations, and economies. The complexity of modern finance means that one breach in a single organization can cascade across an entire network of institutions. This interconnectedness makes collective responsibility non-negotiable. Banks, fintechs, regulators, and technology providers must all work together to share knowledge, detect threats, and respond rapidly.

In developing the structure of this book, I drew upon years of collaboration with industry experts, regulators, and data scientists who believe that progress and protection can coexist. The future of finance will not be defined solely by the speed of innovation but by the strength of its safeguards. Financial systems that are transparent, resilient, and secure will outlast those built on speed alone.

My hope is that readers will finish this book not only with a clearer understanding of financial cybersecurity but also with a renewed sense of purpose. We each have a role to play in shaping the safety of the digital economy. Whether you are writing policy, designing algorithms, approving budgets, or managing client data, the choices you make will define the integrity of tomorrow's financial systems.

The age of digital finance is still being written. Its success will depend on whether we can innovate responsibly and protect diligently. The ideas and frameworks in this book are meant to inspire that balance, to show that financial growth and cybersecurity are not opposing goals but two sides of the same coin.

CHAPTER 1

The New Security Paradigm in the Cloud Era

The modern financial world is built on an invisible promise: that every transaction, every digital exchange of value, is safe. People transfer money, pay bills, and invest through systems they cannot see and rarely understand, yet they trust those systems completely. This trust is the lifeblood of finance, and it is guarded by one discipline above all others, cybersecurity. Without it, innovation would be chaos, and financial growth would rest on quicksand.

Financial cybersecurity exists to preserve the integrity of systems that are now almost entirely digital. From international wire transfers to mobile banking applications, the machinery of modern finance runs on code, and that code is constantly under threat. Criminal groups, nation-state actors, and opportunistic hackers target banks and fintech platforms because that is where data and money converge. As technology advances, so do the methods of attack, and each advancement forces the financial industry to rethink its defenses. Cybersecurity has therefore evolved from a technical afterthought to a strategic imperative, woven into every decision that shapes the future of finance.

At the core of cybersecurity are three enduring principles: confidentiality, integrity, and availability. Confidentiality protects information from unauthorized eyes, ensuring that sensitive data such as account numbers, customer records, and transaction histories remain private. Integrity maintains accuracy, preventing malicious alteration of information that could compromise reporting or decision-making. Availability guarantees that systems and data remain accessible when needed because an unavailable system in finance can cripple entire markets. Together, these principles form the foundation of trust. They represent not just technical ideals but ethical commitments, the assurance that customers' financial lives are handled with care, precision, and transparency.

To understand the weight of cybersecurity in finance, one must consider the transformation of the financial system itself. In the early days of banking, transactions were slow, physical, and largely local. Fraud existed, but it moved at the pace of paper. The introduction of electronic banking changed everything. Networks replaced ledgers, and automation replaced manual verification. Convenience grew, but so did exposure. When ATMs, online banking, and later mobile apps became standard, the attack surface expanded exponentially. Every new connection—between a customer's phone and a bank's server, between an international payment gateway and a local vendor, created new entry points for exploitation. Technology gave the world unprecedented financial access, but it also built a playground for cybercriminals.

The financial industry soon discovered that technology alone could not keep pace with threats. Firewalls, antivirus software, and encryption were necessary, but not sufficient. Breaches still occurred, sometimes from outside attacks and sometimes from within. The human factor, employees clicking on phishing links, executives using weak passwords, contractors misconfiguring servers, proved to be the most unpredictable vulnerability. Institutions that once believed security was a technical department's concern began to recognize it as a collective responsibility. This realization marked the beginning of what experts call a security-first culture, an organizational mindset where every decision, from policy to product design, considers its security implications.

A culture of cybersecurity does not emerge by accident. It is cultivated through leadership, education, and accountability. Financial institutions that take cybersecurity seriously invest heavily in awareness programs, not as compliance formalities but as continuous learning initiatives. Employees are trained to identify suspicious activity, respond appropriately to potential breaches, and understand the value of the data they handle. When staff at every level see security as part of their professional identity rather than a set of restrictions, the organization gains resilience. Such resilience, however, also requires leadership from the top. Boards of directors and chief executives must view cybersecurity not as a cost but as an investment in the institution's longevity. A single breach can cost millions of dollars and years of reputation, yet many of those incidents are preventable through consistent oversight and strategic funding.

Beneath the human framework of awareness lies a vast technological architecture that keeps financial data secure. Institutions deploy multiple layers of defense, a concept known as defense in depth. This approach assumes that no single control is perfect; instead, a series of overlapping protections ensures that if one barrier fails, others remain intact. The first layer often involves firewalls that filter traffic between trusted and untrusted networks. Behind them are intrusion detection systems that monitor unusual activity, endpoint protection tools that safeguard individual devices, and encryption methods that protect data both in storage and in motion. Even if a hacker gains access to a network, encrypted data remains useless without the proper decryption keys. Layered defense reflects a simple truth: perfection in security is impossible, but preparedness is not.

Regulation provides another pillar of the cybersecurity foundation. In finance, compliance is not merely a bureaucratic requirement; it is a guarantee of discipline. International standards such as the General Data Protection Regulation and the Payment Card Industry Data Security Standard set universal expectations for data protection and transaction security. These frameworks compel institutions to maintain accountability through audits, reporting, and breach notification requirements. In Nigeria, the Nigeria Data Protection Regulation and Central Bank of Nigeria guidelines play similar roles, ensuring that banks and fintechs uphold ethical standards in handling personal and financial information. Regulatory adherence shields not only customers but also the institutions themselves. When compliance is taken seriously, it fosters consistency, transparency, and a culture of responsibility across the sector.

Yet, regulation alone cannot eliminate risk. Cyber threats evolve faster than legal reforms, and no law can predict every emerging technology. Financial institutions must therefore combine compliance with foresight. They must anticipate new vulnerabilities in areas such as digital identity, decentralized finance, and real-time payments. This is where innovation becomes a double-edged sword: the same artificial intelligence that enables predictive analytics and automated trading can also power sophisticated fraud schemes. The same blockchain networks that promise transparency can be exploited through coding flaws or insider manipulation. Progress brings exposure, and cybersecurity professionals must learn to evolve as rapidly as the innovations they safeguard.

The cost of failing to do so is steep. Studies consistently show that the financial sector remains the most targeted industry for cyberattacks. The motivation is clear: data and money are directly convertible into power. In 2022 alone, global financial losses from cybercrime exceeded six trillion dollars, a figure projected to double within five years if current trends continue. The economic logic of cybersecurity, therefore, is unambiguous.

Investing in prevention is far less expensive than paying for recovery. Beyond money, breaches destroy reputation and erode public confidence. Customers who lose trust rarely return, and investors withdraw from institutions that cannot protect their data. Cybersecurity, then, is not a defensive posture; it is a strategic advantage.

Resilience has emerged as the new standard of excellence in cybersecurity. No system can promise absolute safety, but resilient systems can withstand shocks and recover quickly. In the financial context, resilience means continuity. It is the ability of banks, markets, and fintech platforms to maintain essential operations even during a breach or outage. Institutions achieve this by developing incident response plans, maintaining secure backups, and practicing recovery drills that simulate real-world attacks. The focus has shifted from mere defense to adaptability. The question is no longer "Will we be attacked?" but "How quickly can we recover and what will we learn from it?" A resilient organization accepts that breaches will happen and turns each one into an opportunity for growth and refinement.

Leadership plays a decisive role in shaping this resilience. The modern Chief Information Security Officer must not only understand technology but also communicate its implications in terms that boards and investors can understand. Cybersecurity decisions affect financial stability, customer satisfaction, and corporate reputation, so they belong at the highest levels of strategy. Forward-thinking leaders integrate cybersecurity metrics into key performance indicators and link them to business outcomes. They understand that protecting data is not separate from growing revenue; it is essential to it. True leadership in cybersecurity means guiding the organization through uncertainty with honesty, adaptability, and an unrelenting focus on trust.

Trust is the thread that ties every concept in financial cybersecurity together. Customers trust institutions to protect their assets. Institutions trust regulators to set fair and consistent standards. Regulators trust technology providers to maintain integrity in the tools they build. When any part of this trust chain breaks, the consequences ripple across the system. A data breach at one bank can trigger panic withdrawals at others. A vulnerability in one payment platform can disrupt global commerce. This interdependence means that cybersecurity is not an individual responsibility but a collective one. Collaboration among banks, fintechs, government agencies, and cybersecurity professionals is no longer optional; it is the only sustainable path forward.

The ethical dimension of cybersecurity cannot be overstated. Financial data carries intimate details of people's lives—income, spending habits, savings goals, and investments. Mishandling or misusing this data is not just a regulatory offense; it is a violation of human dignity. Ethical leadership requires transparency when breaches occur, accountability in governance, and respect for privacy as a fundamental right. Ethical lapses, even when unintentional, erode the moral foundation upon which financial institutions depend. Thus, cybersecurity professionals must not only be skilled in coding and risk analysis but also guided by integrity.

Looking ahead, the financial sector faces both promise and peril. Technologies such as quantum computing, artificial intelligence, and decentralized finance are rewriting the rules of engagement. Quantum computing may one day render current encryption methods obsolete, while artificial intelligence may make both fraud detection and fraud execution faster than ever before. The institutions that will thrive are those that see cybersecurity as a living discipline—one that must evolve, experiment, and learn continuously. The foundations discussed in this chapter will remain relevant, but their application must become more dynamic, adaptive, and forward-thinking.

In the final analysis, the foundation of financial cybersecurity rests on a simple yet profound truth: technology will always change, but trust must remain constant. Protecting that trust requires knowledge, vigilance, and humility. It requires recognizing that every innovation carries risk and that every risk carries an opportunity to strengthen our defenses. The future of finance belongs to those who understand that cybersecurity is not a wall around progress but the bridge that allows it to move safely forward. The world's financial systems are only as secure as the people and principles that guard them, and those who master that understanding will define the next era of global economic confidence.

1.1 The Role of Artificial Intelligence in Foundational Security Systems

The future of financial cybersecurity is increasingly intelligent. Artificial intelligence has become one of the most transformative forces in detecting and mitigating cyber threats before they manifest. Traditional security tools depend on predefined rules and human oversight, but modern financial systems generate data at a volume and speed that far exceed human capacity. Banks process millions of transactions per second, each with distinct patterns, time stamps, and behavioral markers. Within this digital chaos, fraud attempts often hide in plain sight. Artificial intelligence brings the capacity to identify those hidden anomalies through machine learning models trained to recognize subtle irregularities in user behavior and system activity.

In practice, AI-powered threat detection works by continuously learning from both historical and live data. For example, if a user typically logs in from Lagos during business hours and suddenly attempts a transaction from another continent at midnight, the system can flag it as suspicious. Similarly, AI models can detect unusual spending patterns that may indicate card compromise or insider manipulation. These technologies extend beyond detection; they also predict potential vulnerabilities by simulating attack scenarios and stress-testing digital infrastructure. Such predictive intelligence allows institutions to address weaknesses proactively rather than reactively.

AI also enhances the automation of incident response. When a breach occurs, every second counts. Automated systems can isolate compromised accounts, block fraudulent transactions, and trigger alerts before human analysts have even confirmed the incident. This speed reduces damage, preserves evidence, and strengthens confidence. The integration of AI into cybersecurity, however, demands careful oversight. Algorithms can develop biases or produce false positives if not properly calibrated. A security system that locks legitimate users out of their accounts can cause as much harm to reputation as a breach itself. Therefore, financial institutions must ensure that AI operates within ethical and transparent frameworks, combining the precision of machines with the judgment of humans.

The synergy between human expertise and artificial intelligence represents the next stage of foundational security. It shifts cybersecurity from a defensive posture to an anticipatory one. Instead of waiting for attacks, institutions can now foresee them. The application of AI will continue to expand as new technologies such as deep learning and neural networks refine their ability to understand patterns beyond human intuition. These systems will not replace cybersecurity professionals but will augment their abilities, freeing them from repetitive analysis and allowing them to focus on strategy, innovation, and governance. The true power of AI lies not in its autonomy but in its partnership with human intelligence, a partnership that forms the cornerstone of modern financial defense.

1.2 Preparing for the Quantum Era in Finance

If artificial intelligence represents the near future of cybersecurity, quantum computing represents the horizon that redefines it completely.

Quantum technology promises extraordinary processing power, capable of solving complex calculations that would take classical computers centuries to complete. These potential carries both promise and peril. For cybersecurity, it introduces what experts call the "quantum paradox": the same technology that can create unbreakable encryption can also destroy existing encryption systems almost instantly.

Current financial infrastructure depends heavily on mathematical problems that are practically unsolvable with today's computing power. Encryption algorithms such as RSA and ECC rely on the difficulty of factoring large prime numbers or solving elliptic curve equations. A sufficiently advanced quantum computer could break these protections in minutes. The implications for finance are profound. Every secure transaction, every digital signature, every confidential communication could theoretically be decrypted, exposing a century's worth of sensitive data.

Preparing for this shift requires a proactive transition toward **quantum-resistant cryptography**, sometimes called post-quantum security. Researchers and central banks worldwide are already developing algorithms that can withstand quantum attacks by relying on new mathematical foundations. Financial institutions cannot wait for the technology to arrive before acting. Migration to quantum-safe systems takes years, and early adopters will define the standards that protect global finance in the next era.

Beyond cryptography, quantum computing also presents opportunities for strengthening security. Quantum key distribution, a method that uses quantum mechanics to transmit encryption keys, ensures that any interception attempt is immediately detectable. This technology introduces a new dimension of trust, one rooted not in mathematical complexity but in the physical laws of the universe. Financial institutions experimenting with this approach are already demonstrating that the future of trust may depend on science as much as on policy.

The emergence of quantum technology will demand a new mindset within financial cybersecurity. Institutions must begin to think in decades rather than quarters, anticipating how foundational security principles will adapt to new realities. Investment in research, partnerships with universities, and participation in global standard-setting bodies will become critical. Those who lead in quantum readiness will not only secure their systems but also shape the next generation of financial infrastructure. The challenge is monumental, but so was the shift from paper to digital banking. History has shown that finance evolves not by avoiding risk but by preparing for it wisely.

CHAPTER TWO

Anatomy of Financial Fraud and Digital Threats

Fraud has always existed wherever money exists. In the physical world, it took the form of forged signatures, counterfeit currencies, or deceptive accounting. In the digital world, it has evolved into something far more invisible and far more dangerous. Modern financial fraud does not always require a weapon or a disguise. It requires access; access to systems, identities, or trust. What makes digital fraud particularly insidious is its ability to travel across borders, replicate itself in seconds, and disguise its origins behind layers of code and anonymity. The anatomy of financial fraud today reveals an ecosystem of threats that is complex, adaptive, and constantly evolving alongside the technologies it exploits.

Every act of financial fraud begins with intent and opportunity. Attackers, whether individuals or organized groups, study systems in the same way investors study markets. They look for weak points, behavioral patterns, and timing. They exploit human tendencies such as haste, overconfidence, or fear, and combine them with technological weaknesses. In this interplay of human psychology and digital engineering, the line between deception and innovation is often thin. The same creativity that fuels legitimate fintech breakthroughs also fuels fraudulent innovation. Understanding the anatomy of these attacks requires examining not just how they occur, but why they continue to succeed despite the billions spent to prevent them.

One of the oldest and most prevalent forms of financial fraud in the digital age is phishing. It relies not on breaking systems, but on manipulating people. Phishing attacks mimic legitimate communication from banks, payment platforms, or government agencies. They persuade users to reveal sensitive information such as passwords, card numbers, or one-time verification codes. The sophistication of phishing has grown to a point where even seasoned professionals struggle to distinguish real messages from forged ones. Attackers now use artificial intelligence to craft convincing emails, replicate institutional websites, and even mimic the tone and grammar of official correspondence. The result is a form of fraud that bypasses technology altogether and targets human trust directly.

Closely related is **vishing** (voice phishing), in which fraudsters impersonate bank representatives or security officers over the phone. They often combine personal data gathered from social media with psychological manipulation to pressure victims into immediate action. Similarly, **smishing**, or SMS-based phishing, exploits mobile convenience to deliver malicious links. In an environment where customers expect instant communication and rapid transactions, these scams thrive on urgency. A single deceptive message can lead to thousands of compromised accounts within hours.

Beyond these socially engineered attacks lies the realm of **identity theft**, the cornerstone of digital financial crime. Here, attackers steal personal data from databases, online forms, or compromised applications, using it to impersonate victims or open fraudulent accounts. With the proliferation of data breaches, vast quantities of personal information now circulate in underground markets known as the dark web. Names, addresses, national identification numbers, and biometric data are traded like commodities.

Once purchased, these data sets are used to create synthetic identities; fictional personas built from fragments of real information. Synthetic identity fraud is especially dangerous because it can bypass automated credit scoring and identity verification systems, allowing criminals to establish legitimacy before committing large-scale fraud.

Financial institutions face another persistent threat in **account takeover attacks**, where cybercriminals gain control of legitimate user accounts through stolen credentials or session hijacking. Once inside, they perform unauthorized transactions, alter account details, and transfer funds before detection. The rise of mobile banking has intensified this risk, as users frequently access financial platforms from unsecured networks or devices. Attackers exploit these vulnerabilities using malware, keyloggers, and credential stuffing techniques, testing stolen passwords across multiple services until they find a match. This phenomenon is particularly alarming because it relies on a simple human habit, password reuse.

While consumer-targeted attacks attract headlines, institutional fraud poses equally grave risks. In this category, attackers target the financial infrastructure itself rather than its users. Examples include fraudulent wire transfers, manipulation of internal systems, and infiltration of payment networks. The Bangladesh Bank heist of 2016 stands as a historic case study. Hackers infiltrated the bank's network, obtained legitimate credentials, and sent fraudulent transfer requests through the SWIFT interbank messaging system. They attempted to steal nearly one billion dollars and succeeded in moving eighty-one million before detection. The heist exposed how even highly regulated systems, when combined with human error and procedural lapses, could be manipulated with precision and patience.

Another rising form of digital fraud involves **ransomware**, a category of malicious software designed to encrypt an organization's data and demand payment for its release. Financial institutions are prime targets due to the sensitivity and urgency of their operations. When a bank's systems are locked, every minute translates to potential loss. Attackers exploit this urgency, demanding payment in cryptocurrencies to avoid traceability. Ransomware groups now operate as organized businesses, offering "Ransomware-as-a-Service" kits on the dark web, complete with customer support and profit-sharing models. The evolution of ransomware illustrates a larger truth about cybercrime; it has become industrialized.

Beyond direct attacks, there are also **insider threats**, which remain one of the most difficult to detect. Insiders include employees, contractors, or partners who misuse their authorized access for personal gain or malicious intent. In some cases, they act alone; in others, they collaborate with external attackers. Insiders can manipulate transaction records, leak customer data, or disable security controls. Their actions are often motivated by financial distress, revenge, or coercion. Unlike external attackers, insiders operate within trusted systems, making their detection far more complex. Institutions must therefore strike a delicate balance between operational efficiency and surveillance, ensuring that oversight does not compromise privacy or trust among staff.

The digitalization of finance has also given rise to new arenas of fraud such as cryptocurrency scams, fake investment platforms, and decentralized finance (DeFi) exploits. While blockchain technology itself is secure, the platforms built on top of it are often rushed to market without sufficient testing or auditing. Fraudulent initial coin offerings (ICOs), rug pulls, and smart contract vulnerabilities have led to billions in losses. In 2022 alone, blockchain analysis firms estimated that DeFi-related hacks and scams accounted for more than half of all crypto thefts worldwide. Attackers exploit the transparency of blockchain to study protocols, identify weak coding logic, and execute attacks that drain liquidity pools within seconds. The irony of decentralized systems is that their openness, which was meant to democratize finance, also exposes them to manipulation by those with technical expertise and malicious intent.

To counter these evolving threats, financial institutions must adopt layered, intelligence-driven strategies. Fraud detection today relies heavily on behavioral analytics, pattern recognition, and real-time monitoring. Artificial intelligence can learn from millions of legitimate transactions to identify deviations that signal potential fraud. However, technology alone is not enough. Cybercriminals continuously adapt their methods to evade detection, forcing institutions to evolve equally fast. Collaboration between banks, regulators, and technology providers is essential. Shared intelligence networks allow the early identification of emerging attack patterns and enable collective defense responses. In recent years, several national and regional cybersecurity alliances have been established for precisely this purpose, to make threat intelligence a shared resource rather than a private advantage.

Regulation and compliance frameworks play a parallel role in fraud prevention. The introduction of Know Your Customer (KYC) and Anti-Money Laundering (AML) policies has significantly reduced the anonymity that fraudsters exploit. Yet, the same regulations can create friction in user experience if implemented rigidly. The challenge for institutions is to design compliance processes that are both rigorous and user-friendly. Biometric authentication, digital identity verification, and AI-assisted risk scoring represent promising solutions. These technologies not only improve fraud detection but also reduce false positives that frustrate legitimate customers. In a financial ecosystem where speed and security must coexist, achieving this balance is both art and science.

Fraud prevention, however, does not end with detection; it extends into response and recovery. Institutions must be prepared to act decisively when fraud occurs. Incident response teams, forensic investigators, and communication specialists must collaborate to contain damage, restore systems, and maintain public confidence. Transparency plays a crucial role here. Concealing fraud incidents, as some institutions have attempted in the past, often leads to greater loss of trust than the fraud itself. The public understands that breaches can happen; what matters is how an institution responds. Swift acknowledgment, clear communication, and visible corrective measures restore credibility far more effectively than silence.

What makes financial fraud particularly challenging is its evolving nature. Each advancement in security breeds a new generation of deception. Attackers are increasingly turning to artificial intelligence themselves, using deepfake audio to impersonate executives or automated bots to flood systems with synthetic transactions. The battle between defenders and attackers has thus become an arms race of intelligence. The winners will be those who adapt the fastest not only in technology but also to the mindset. A truly secure institution is one that treats every employee as part of the defense mechanism, every policy as a living document, and every incident as a lesson rather than a failure.

Financial fraud, in all its forms, is not merely a technical issue but a human one. It reveals the constant tension between trust and temptation, between progress and vulnerability. As financial systems become more interconnected and digital identities replace physical ones, the cost of misplaced trust will continue to rise. Understanding the anatomy of these threats is the first step toward controlling them. The next step, which this book will continue to explore, is building systems so resilient that even when attacked, they bend without breaking and adapt without losing their integrity. In that adaptation lies the true art of cybersecurity not the elimination of risk, but the mastery of response.

2.1 The Economics and Psychology of Digital Fraud

Behind every cyberattack is an economy, and behind every fraudulent economy is human motivation. Financial fraud has become a global business powered by incentives that mirror legitimate industries. There are organized hierarchies, service providers, customer support channels, and even performance bonuses in the world of digital crime. Dark web markets function like e-commerce platforms, offering stolen data, malware kits, and fake digital identities for sale. Buyers leave reviews and ratings for sellers, and transactions are conducted through escrow services in cryptocurrency. What once seemed like isolated acts of hacking has matured into a structured underground economy that thrives on efficiency and demand.

Understanding this economy helps explain why cybercrime continues to grow despite the advancement of security technologies. Fraud, like any business, follows the principle of profit versus effort. Attackers invest in the tools and methods that yield the highest returns for the least resistance. They exploit systems not because they are passionate about technology but because they see financial systems as predictable, scalable markets. This economic rationality also extends to the outsourcing of cybercrime. A skilled hacker no longer needs to execute every stage of an attack. Specialized services now exist for phishing campaigns, botnet rentals, and data laundering. This compartmentalization allows cybercriminals to operate like corporations, dividing labor and risk while maximizing efficiency.

Yet, beyond economics, there is psychology, the cognitive and emotional dimension of digital fraud. Human error remains the primary gateway for most breaches. The success of social engineering attacks lies not in complex code but in exploiting predictable human reactions: curiosity, urgency, greed, and fear. Fraudsters study behavioral patterns and tailor their attacks to trigger these instincts. For instance, emails about account suspension or fake transaction alerts exploit fear and urgency, prompting users to act before thinking. Investment scams exploit greed, offering unrealistic returns and playing on the universal desire for quick gain. In many cases, victims of fraud are not careless but human. Understanding this truth reshapes how financial institutions train their staff and customers. Security awareness programs must now include elements of psychology, teaching people to recognize manipulation as much as malware.

The psychology of fraud also extends to the perpetrators. Some cybercriminals view themselves not as thieves but as disruptors of an unjust system. Others rationalize their actions as intelligence tests or expressions of skill. The anonymity of the internet dissolves moral boundaries, creating an illusion of harmlessness. For policymakers and educators, addressing this mindset is as important as strengthening firewalls. Nations that invest in digital literacy and ethical technology education build not only a workforce capable of defending against cyber threats but also one less likely to create them. Combating financial fraud, therefore, requires engaging both the rational and emotional aspects of human behavior; the economy that drives it and the psychology that sustains it.

2.2 The Future Landscape of Financial Threats

The evolution of fraud is inseparable from the evolution of technology. Every innovation in financial convenience brings with it a new category of risk. The next decade will see a convergence of technologies; artificial intelligence, quantum computing, biometrics, and the Internet of Things — that will redefine both the power and the vulnerability of digital finance. These technologies promise efficiency and inclusion but also amplify the consequences of oversight.

One of the most imminent challenges is the weaponization of artificial intelligence. Fraudsters are already using AI to generate synthetic identities, manipulate biometric systems, and craft convincing deepfake audio or video messages that impersonate corporate executives. In 2020, a well-documented case in Europe involved criminals using deepfake voice technology to impersonate a CEO and authorize a fraudulent transfer exceeding two hundred thousand dollars. Such attacks demonstrate that the line between authenticity and deception is thinning. As machine learning models become more sophisticated, detecting fraud will require algorithms that can understand context and intent rather than simply pattern deviations.

Another looming threat is the rise of **quantum decryption**, discussed briefly in the previous chapter. While quantum computing holds immense potential for innovation, it also poses an existential risk to current encryption methods. A single quantum breakthrough could render much of today's financial security obsolete, exposing stored data and encrypted transactions to instant decryption. Institutions must therefore invest in quantum-safe cryptographic solutions now, long before quantum computing becomes commercially viable. The transition to post-quantum algorithms will be one of the most significant shifts in the history of cybersecurity, requiring global coordination and massive infrastructural adaptation.

The expansion of **open banking** and **API-driven ecosystems** introduces another layer of vulnerability. Open banking allows third-party providers to access consumer financial data securely to build innovative services. However, every new integration point expands the potential attack surface. A weak link in one service can expose data across multiple institutions. Regulators will need to strengthen frameworks for API governance, authentication standards, and liability distribution to prevent systemic risks. Similarly, as financial data becomes more decentralized, the concept of perimeter security — defending a defined boundary — will become obsolete. Cybersecurity in the future will depend on zero-trust models that verify every interaction, regardless of source.

Emerging economies face unique challenges in this evolving threat landscape. The rapid adoption of fintech solutions in Africa, Asia, and Latin America has accelerated inclusion but also outpaced regulation. Many startups operate with limited cybersecurity budgets and rely heavily on third-party infrastructure. This creates dependency chains that few understand fully. A single misconfiguration in a cloud environment or an unpatched vulnerability in a software library can cascade across thousands of users. Building resilience in these markets will require not only technology but also policy; frameworks that make security funding, compliance, and capacity-building integral to innovation.

The future of financial threats is not only about technology but also about narrative. Fraudsters are increasingly using misinformation and digital manipulation to erode trust in financial institutions. Fake news about bank insolvency, manipulated screenshots of payment failures, or false social media campaigns can spark panic withdrawals and destabilize markets. Information warfare, once a concern of politics, now threatens finance directly. Defending against such threats requires integrating cybersecurity with communication strategy and public education. The most secure system can still fail if users no longer believe in it.

The concept of fraud itself may evolve. As artificial intelligence systems handle more of the financial decision-making process, new forms of manipulation will emerge; targeting algorithms rather than humans. Adversarial attacks, where malicious actors subtly alter data to mislead machine learning models, could distort credit scoring, investment predictions, or fraud detection itself. The battleground will shift from systems of data storage to systems of data interpretation. The winners of that battle will be those who learn not only to secure data but also to secure meaning.

CHAPTER THREE

Risk Management Frameworks and Compliance in Finance

Every financial system is built on the idea of balance; between risk and reward, opportunity and control, ambition and caution. Cybersecurity operates within this same balance. The more digital a financial institution becomes, the more exposed it is to threats that can undermine its stability. Managing that exposure is not about eliminating risk but about understanding, anticipating, and minimizing its potential impact. This is the philosophy that underpins risk management in the financial world.

Risk management in cybersecurity is both art and science. It begins with the recognition that not all risks are equal. Some are predictable and manageable, while others are unpredictable and disruptive. Financial institutions face threats ranging from minor software vulnerabilities to systemic disruptions that can destabilize markets. Each requires a different level of response and governance. The challenge lies in designing a framework that can accommodate complexity without collapsing under it. The strongest institutions are those that treat risk management not as an annual exercise but as an evolving discipline, a living system of protection and adaptability.

A mature risk management framework begins with **risk identification**. This involves cataloguing every potential source of threat, whether technological, human, environmental, or procedural. In digital finance, risks often arise from misconfigurations, outdated software, weak access controls, and vendor dependencies. For example, a third-party payment processor might become the weakest link in an otherwise secure ecosystem. Identifying these risks requires visibility, and visibility requires collaboration across departments. Cybersecurity cannot operate in isolation from business units, compliance officers, or data scientists. Each contributes a unique understanding of the institution's vulnerabilities. Together, they form the map that guides all subsequent actions.

Once risks are identified, the next phase is assessment and prioritization. This is where financial institutions measure the likelihood of each risk and its potential impact. The goal is to distinguish between low-level threats that can be tolerated and critical risks that require immediate intervention. Quantitative assessments use statistical models, historical data, and simulation techniques to assign numerical values to risks. Qualitative assessments, on the other hand, rely on expert judgment and contextual understanding. In practice, both methods work best when combined. A bank may use predictive analytics to estimate the probability of cyber fraud but still depend on human analysis to interpret the socio-political context behind that risk.

Following assessment comes **risk mitigation**, the process of designing controls to reduce exposure. These controls can be technical, procedural, or strategic. Technical controls include encryption, firewalls, intrusion detection, and access management. Procedural controls include policies, training programs, and periodic audits. Strategic controls involve diversification, cyber insurance, and crisis management planning. Effective mitigation requires proportionality. Institutions must match the strength of their defenses to the sensitivity of the assets they protect.

Overprotection can drain resources, while under protection invites catastrophe. The art lies in aligning defense mechanisms with both operational needs and regulatory expectations.

At the center of modern financial security is the concept of **governance, risk, and compliance (GRC)**. GRC is more than a framework; it is a philosophy that integrates cybersecurity with business objectives. Governance establishes accountability, defining who is responsible for what. Risk management ensures that those responsibilities are executed with foresight. Compliance ensures that execution aligns with legal and ethical standards. Together, they create a unified ecosystem of control. In well-governed institutions, cybersecurity is embedded in decision-making, budgeting, and strategy. It is not a reactive department but a proactive business partner. When an organization reaches this level of maturity, cybersecurity becomes part of its DNA.

Compliance remains one of the most critical elements of financial cybersecurity. In a world where data is global but laws are national, compliance provides the bridge between innovation and accountability. Regulations such as the General Data Protection Regulation (GDPR), Payment Card Industry Data Security Standard (PCI DSS), and ISO 27001 define minimum standards for data protection and risk management. In Nigeria, frameworks such as the Nigeria Data Protection Regulation (NDPR), the Central Bank of Nigeria (CBN) Risk-Based Cybersecurity Framework, and the National Information Technology Development Agency (NITDA) Guidelines serve similar purposes. These standards compel institutions to protect consumer data, report breaches, and maintain operational resilience.

However, compliance is often misunderstood. Many institutions treat it as a checklist; something to be passed during audits or inspections. This approach reduces compliance to formality rather than culture. True compliance is continuous. It evolves with the business model and the threat landscape. For instance, GDPR does not simply require companies to protect personal data; it requires them to demonstrate accountability through documentation and transparency. PCI DSS does not merely mandate encryption; it demands continuous risk assessment and system testing. Compliance, when practiced correctly, becomes a framework for trust. It tells customers, regulators, and investors that an institution values integrity as much as profit.

A significant evolution in compliance thinking has been the shift toward **risk-based regulation**. Traditionally, regulators imposed uniform controls regardless of an institution's size, complexity, or risk profile. This one-size-fits-all approach often led to inefficiencies. Risk-based frameworks, however, prioritize flexibility and proportionality. They allow institutions to tailor their controls based on specific exposures. For example, a regional microfinance bank may not require the same cybersecurity infrastructure as a multinational investment firm, but both must achieve the same outcome, the protection of data and financial stability. The Central Bank of Nigeria's cybersecurity guidelines reflect this philosophy by emphasizing adaptive risk management rather than rigid adherence.

Beyond technical and regulatory aspects, the culture of compliance depends on leadership and tone from the top. Executives and board members must treat cybersecurity reports with the same seriousness as financial statements. Decisions about mergers, acquisitions, and digital transformation should include risk assessments as mandatory inputs. The alignment of cybersecurity with corporate strategy ensures that security is not viewed as a cost center but as a value driver. Financial institutions that have embraced this mindset often outperform their peers in both customer retention and market confidence. Trust, once again, proves to be the most valuable currency.

Another essential component of financial risk management is **incident response and business continuity planning**. Even the most compliant organization can experience a breach. What distinguishes resilient institutions is their ability to respond quickly and effectively. An incident response plan defines roles, communication channels, and recovery steps for various scenarios. It ensures that during a crisis, decisions are made with clarity, not panic. Business continuity planning extends this logic to operational recovery, ensuring that essential services continue even in the face of disruption. For instance, during the 2017 WannaCry ransomware attack, organizations with pre-tested recovery protocols restored operations within hours, while others suffered days of paralysis. Preparedness does not eliminate crisis, but it transforms its impact.

Risk management also extends beyond organizational boundaries. The rise of third-party risk has become one of the most pressing challenges in financial cybersecurity. Banks and fintechs increasingly depend on external vendors for cloud hosting, payment processing, data analytics, and customer support. Each partnership introduces dependencies that can either strengthen or weaken security. Recent years have witnessed multiple high-profile breaches that originated not from the primary institution but from third-party providers. Managing these risks requires continuous monitoring, contractual safeguards, and collaborative accountability. Institutions must ensure that their partners meet or exceed their own security standards. In the era of interconnected finance, no organization is safer than its weakest link.

Modern risk management also involves leveraging technology for automation and intelligence. Machine learning tools can now predict potential vulnerabilities, simulate attack paths, and quantify the potential financial impact of cyber incidents. Predictive analytics transforms risk management from a static reporting function into a dynamic forecasting engine. Automation reduces human error, speeds up compliance checks, and enables real-time adjustments to security posture. Yet, technology is only as effective as the people who design and interpret it. The human oversight of automated systems ensures that decisions remain ethical, contextually relevant, and aligned with institutional values.

The future of risk management in finance lies in convergence; the merging of cybersecurity, enterprise risk, and regulatory compliance into a single strategic framework. As digital finance continues to evolve, too will the risks that accompany it. New payment architectures, digital currencies, and decentralized finance models will challenge traditional definitions of control. Institutions must therefore move beyond compliance to embrace **resilience governance**, a model that focuses on continuous learning, adaptive policies, and transparent communication. In this new paradigm, regulation is not an obstacle to innovation but a partner in progress.

Ultimately, the purpose of risk management and compliance is not fear but confidence. It gives institutions the assurance to innovate responsibly and customers the peace of mind to engage freely. When risk management functions as an enabler rather than a constraint, it transforms cybersecurity from a cost to a competitive advantage. The financial institutions that will thrive in the next decade are those that recognize that every risk is a lesson, every regulation and opportunity, and every act of compliance an investment in trust. In that realization lies the quiet strength of secure finance; a system that protects not only data and assets but the very belief that progress and safety can coexist.

3.1 Cyber Insurance and Financial Risk Transfer

No matter how strong a financial institution's cybersecurity posture may be, risk can never be completely eliminated. There will always be unforeseen vulnerabilities, human errors, and zero-day exploits that slip through the most advanced defenses. Recognizing this reality, the global financial industry has increasingly turned to **cyber insurance** as a mechanism for risk transfer. Unlike traditional insurance, which covers tangible losses such as property damage or physical theft, cyber insurance deals with the intangible costs of digital compromise — data breaches, ransomware attacks, regulatory fines, reputational harm, and business interruption.

The rationale behind cyber insurance is straightforward: to convert unpredictable cybersecurity losses into manageable financial exposure. It provides organizations with a safety net that absorbs part of the economic shock after a breach. For example, if a ransomware attack forces a bank offline for several days, cyber insurance can cover the costs of system restoration, legal defense, and customer notification. However, the growing complexity of digital threats has made underwriting such policies increasingly difficult. Insurers now face the same challenge as the institutions they protect assessing risk in an environment where threats evolve faster than data models can predict.

For insurance providers, this has led to the emergence of **data-driven underwriting**. Premiums are no longer calculated solely based on company size or sector but on measurable cybersecurity maturity. Insurers examine metrics such as patch management, employee training, encryption standards, and incident response capabilities before determining coverage terms. In some regions, insurers even require third-party audits to validate an applicant's security controls. This shift has had an unintended yet beneficial consequence: it incentivizes better cybersecurity practices. Institutions that maintain high standards of compliance and governance are rewarded with lower premiums, creating a financial motivation for security excellence.

Despite its growing importance, cyber insurance is not a substitute for risk management; it is a complement. The existence of coverage does not absolve organizations from their duty to prevent and detect incidents. In fact, insurers often reject claims arising from negligence or failure to adhere to basic security protocols. The relationship between insurer and insured therefore becomes one of shared accountability. Both parties must continuously assess emerging risks and adapt policies accordingly. As the market matures, standardized policy language, clearer definitions of cyber events, and cooperative data sharing will become essential for maintaining trust in this form of protection.

The future of cyber insurance lies in collaboration between the public and private sectors. Governments and regulators are beginning to explore frameworks for national cyber risk pools that distribute losses from catastrophic digital events across multiple insurers and industries. Similar to how natural disaster insurance works, this model would prevent systemic financial collapse following a large-scale cyberattack. For financial institutions, participation in such frameworks will not only provide protection but also reinforce public confidence. Cyber insurance, when combined with strong governance and resilient infrastructure, transforms cybersecurity from an operational cost into a strategic safeguard for national and global stability.

3.2 Ethical Governance and the Evolution of Regulation

Every regulation is a reflection of its time. The laws that once governed financial integrity were designed for a world of paper transactions and physical vaults. Today, value moves at the speed of light across invisible networks, and those old frameworks can no longer contain it. As financial systems evolve, so too must their regulations. The next frontier of compliance lies not merely in enforcing existing standards but in anticipating the ethical challenges that emerging technologies bring.

Ethical governance begins with transparency. Customers and regulators alike demand to know how financial institutions collect, process, and store data. This demand has intensified with the rise of artificial intelligence in credit scoring, fraud detection, and customer analytics. Algorithms can make decisions that affect millions of lives, yet the logic behind those decisions is often opaque. Regulators now expect institutions to adopt **algorithmic accountability**, ensuring that automated systems are explainable, unbiased, and auditable. Ethical governance therefore extends beyond data protection to include fairness, equity, and human oversight in technological design.

The convergence of technology and ethics is also reshaping how compliance officers approach regulation. Traditionally, compliance has been retrospective; institutions acted, and regulators responded. The new paradigm is regulation by design, where ethical and legal principles are embedded into technology from its inception. This proactive approach ensures that innovation and compliance grow together rather than in conflict. For example, open banking frameworks in Europe and Africa now require that APIs not only meet technical specifications but also adhere to ethical data-sharing standards that protect user consent and autonomy. Such measures represent a maturing of the compliance mindset from reactive enforcement to proactive prevention.

International coordination remains one of the greatest challenges in modern regulation. Financial data moves across jurisdictions where privacy laws differ, creating conflicts and loopholes. A transaction initiated in Lagos may be processed through servers in Dublin and verified in Singapore. Which laws apply in such a case? Resolving this ambiguity requires collaboration between regulators through bilateral agreements and transnational frameworks. Organizations such as the Financial Stability Board and the International Organization of Securities Commissions are already working toward harmonized cybersecurity standards. However, implementation remains uneven. Some countries enforce strict data sovereignty, while others prioritize innovation freedom. The future of ethical governance will depend on reconciling these competing priorities to ensure that security and privacy remain universal values rather than territorial privileges.

A deeper layer of ethical governance concerns the relationship between institutions and the individuals they serve. Trust is not built by compliance alone but by empathy; the understanding that behind every transaction lies a person whose security and dignity depend on responsible stewardship. Financial institutions hold immense power over data that reveals intimate details about people's lives: their income, habits, aspirations, and vulnerabilities. The ethical use of this information is the moral core of cybersecurity. Institutions that misuse or overexploit customer data may comply with the letter of the law but violate its spirit. True integrity requires restraint, transparency, and respect for privacy as a human right.

As technology continues to advance, regulation will need to become both more dynamic and more principled. Static laws cannot keep pace with quantum computing, artificial intelligence, and decentralized finance. What will endure are the principles of fairness, accountability, and responsibility. The most progressive regulators are those who act as partners in innovation rather than obstacles to it. They recognize that ethical governance and financial growth are not mutually exclusive but mutually reinforcing. Financial institutions that adopt this mindset will find that compliance is not the end of regulation but the beginning of leadership. By aligning security with morality and innovation with accountability, they will shape a financial future that is both prosperous and principled.

CHAPTER FOUR

The Role of Artificial Intelligence in Fraud Detection

In the intricate web of modern finance, fraud detection has become both a science and a race; a contest between those who seek to exploit vulnerabilities and those determined to safeguard trust. As transactions multiply across borders and platforms, the complexity of financial crime has outgrown human capacity. The scale, speed, and sophistication of cyber fraud demand tools that can learn, predict, and adapt faster than any human analyst. This is where artificial intelligence steps in, not as a replacement for human intuition but as its most powerful ally.

Artificial intelligence (AI) has changed the grammar of cybersecurity. It has moved the discipline from reactive defense to predictive resilience. Traditional fraud detection systems relied on static rules; fixed thresholds, defined patterns, and historical precedents. They could detect known schemes but struggled with novel or evolving ones. Fraudsters quickly learned to bypass rule-based systems by introducing slight variations in their techniques. In contrast, AI systems thrive on change. They are designed to learn from every new event, refining their models as they process more data. In a financial ecosystem that processes billions of transactions daily, this capacity for continuous learning has become indispensable.

The cornerstone of AI in fraud detection is **machine learning**; algorithms that analyze data to identify patterns of normal and abnormal behavior. In financial contexts, these systems observe transactional attributes such as amount, location, device type, and frequency. When behavior deviates significantly from a user's established profile, the system raises an alert. Unlike traditional filters that depend on predefined limits, machine learning algorithms evolve organically, learning subtle distinctions between legitimate and fraudulent actions. For instance, they can distinguish between a user's legitimate international travel and a fraudster's unauthorized access by analyzing timing, device fingerprints, and behavioral nuances such as typing rhythm or navigation speed.

A more advanced form of this technology, **deep learning**, allows systems to process complex, unstructured data such as text, voice, or images. Deep learning models can analyze chat logs, transaction notes, or even customer service interactions to detect inconsistencies that might signal fraud. In large institutions where data exists in multiple formats; from emails to payment records — this holistic view provides a unified understanding of risk. AI systems can correlate anomalies across seemingly unrelated channels, identifying fraud patterns invisible to human analysts. For example, a sudden surge in loan applications from a particular region, combined with identical writing styles and contact details, may reveal an organized fraud network.

Another critical development is **natural language processing (NLP)**, which enables AI systems to interpret human communication. Fraudsters often use social engineering through emails, messages, or call transcripts to manipulate individuals into compromising security. NLP models can analyze tone, intent, and linguistic structure to flag deceptive or manipulative language. In compliance functions, NLP helps monitor employee communications for insider threats or policy breaches. These tools have made it possible to extend fraud detection beyond transactional data into the realm of human behavior; the very space where most financial crimes originate.

AI's greatest strength in fraud detection lies in **real-time analysis**. Traditional auditing methods operate after the fact, detecting irregularities only once losses have occurred. AI, however, works in milliseconds. It evaluates transactions as they happen, blocking suspicious activity before damage is done. In global payment systems where funds can move across continents in seconds, this speed is revolutionary. Financial institutions now deploy AI-powered fraud detection engines that score every transaction in real time, weighing hundreds of variables before deciding whether to approve, flag, or deny it. The ability to act instantly transforms cybersecurity from reactive repair to active prevention.

However, the same speed that empowers AI also introduces new challenges. False positives; legitimate transactions wrongly flagged as suspicious can frustrate customers and erode trust. Overzealous systems may block valid payments or freeze accounts without sufficient context. To address this, institutions are adopting adaptive learning models that balance sensitivity with precision. These models refine themselves continuously, learning from analysts' feedback and customer confirmations. The more data they process, the better they become at distinguishing fraud from genuine anomalies. The ideal system learns to be cautious without being paranoid, a difficult equilibrium that defines the maturity of modern AI-driven fraud detection.

Another area of profound impact is behavioral biometrics, where AI studies how individuals interact with devices rather than what credentials they use. Typing speed, mouse movement, screen pressure, and navigation habits form unique behavioral signatures. Even if a fraudster possesses the correct password, the subtle differences in interaction can expose the intrusion. Behavioral biometrics thus shift the paradigm of authentication from "what you know" or "what you have" to "who you are." These invisible patterns of behavior offer a level of security that is both user-friendly and nearly impossible to replicate.

Beyond detection, AI plays a crucial role in **investigation and attribution**. Once a suspicious pattern is detected, the system must determine its source, motive, and scale. AI-powered forensic tools can trace attack paths through vast digital logs, linking activities across multiple systems. They can map relationships between fraudulent accounts, identifying clusters that belong to a single network. This ability to visualize connections transforms investigation from guesswork into data-driven analysis. It allows law enforcement and internal investigators to dismantle entire fraud rings rather than isolated cases.

Despite these advances, the integration of AI into financial security introduces ethical and operational dilemmas. Chief among them is the issue of **algorithmic transparency**. Many AI models, especially deep learning systems, operate as "black boxes," producing results that even their creators struggle to explain. This opacity conflicts with the financial industry's need for accountability. Regulators and auditors require clear explanations for why a transaction was flagged or declined. Institutions must therefore find ways to make AI interpretable without diluting its sophistication. The emerging field of **explainable AI (XAI)** addresses this need by developing models that can justify their decisions in human-understandable terms.

Bias is another concern. AI systems learn from data, and data reflects human behavior; including its prejudices. If historical data contains biases against certain demographics, the AI may unintentionally perpetuate discrimination in fraud detection or credit decisions. A system might, for instance, associate higher fraud risk with particular regions or spending patterns based on skewed data. Ethical AI development requires continuous auditing of training datasets, fairness testing, and inclusive representation. Financial institutions must establish governance frameworks that ensure technology serves all users equitably.

The adoption of AI also raises questions of **accountability and liability**. When an algorithm makes an incorrect decision that leads to financial loss or reputational damage, who bears responsibility, the developer, the institution, or the machine itself? These questions are forcing regulators to rethink legal frameworks around automation and decision-making. In some jurisdictions, institutions must demonstrate "human-in-the-loop" oversight for critical AI systems, ensuring that no high-impact decision occurs without human review. This hybrid model combines machine efficiency with human judgment, preserving accountability while maintaining speed.

As artificial intelligence continues to evolve, it is increasingly being deployed not only within institutions but also across networks. Collaborative intelligence systems now allow banks and fintechs to share anonymized fraud data securely through blockchain or encrypted cloud environments. This collective learning approach strengthens the entire industry. When one institution detects a new fraud pattern, others can preemptively defend against it. In effect, AI transforms cybersecurity from a series of isolated defenses into a coordinated ecosystem. Such cooperation represents a fundamental shift in financial security philosophy; from competition to collaboration in the fight against fraud.

Looking ahead, the future of AI in fraud detection lies in autonomous security systems capable of self-adaptation. These systems will not merely react to threats but anticipate them through predictive modeling, simulating potential attack scenarios before they occur. They will analyze emerging patterns from social media, dark web activity, and global transaction data to foresee shifts in criminal strategy. In doing so, they will act less like static tools and more like digital sentinels; proactive guardians of trust in an unpredictable landscape.

Yet, even as AI becomes more powerful, it must remain guided by human values. Technology may detect patterns, but only people can define purpose. The moral dimension of AI in finance lies in ensuring that the pursuit of efficiency does not eclipse fairness, privacy, or dignity. Institutions that deploy AI with transparency and empathy will not only reduce fraud but also strengthen public confidence in digital systems. In contrast, those that prioritize speed over accountability risk creating a future where trust itself becomes collateral damage.

Artificial intelligence represents the most significant leap in financial security since the advent of digital banking. It gives institutions the ability to see, learn, and act faster than ever before; to transform uncertainty into foresight. But its true success will be measured not by how well it protects data, but by how deeply it preserves integrity. For in the end, AI is not merely about preventing fraud; it is about upholding the promise that technology, when guided by ethics and vision, can make finance not only smarter but safer for all.

4.1 AI in Predictive Risk Modeling

The true genius of artificial intelligence in finance lies not only in its ability to detect fraud after it occurs but in its potential to predict and prevent it before it happens. Predictive risk modeling marks a fundamental shift in how institutions understand security; from historical reaction to real-time foresight. It enables banks, insurance firms, and fintech platforms to anticipate vulnerabilities, prioritize defenses, and allocate resources more intelligently.

Predictive models operate on the principle that fraud leaves footprints, even before it strikes. By analyzing patterns in data, these systems can identify early warning signs that human analysts might overlook. For example, a sudden increase in small, low-value transactions across multiple accounts may appear harmless in isolation. Yet, to a trained machine learning model, such patterns may indicate probing attacks where criminals test system thresholds before attempting larger heists. Similarly, anomalies in login times, device types, or session durations can help predict credential stuffing or account takeover attempts long before they succeed.

Financial institutions are increasingly using supervised and unsupervised learning models to fine-tune these predictive systems. Supervised learning relies on labeled datasets; past examples of legitimate and fraudulent transactions to teach algorithms what fraud looks like. Unsupervised learning, by contrast, searches for irregularities in data without prior examples. It detects novel, emerging fraud patterns that do not match any known category. Together, these techniques provide a comprehensive defense, balancing the precision of experience with the adaptability of discovery.

One of the most promising developments in predictive modeling is the integration of graph analytics. Fraud rarely occurs in isolation; it is almost always part of a network. Graph-based AI models map relationships between users, transactions, and entities to uncover hidden connections. For instance, a series of seemingly independent accounts making transfers to a shared destination may reveal an organized laundering operation. This form of relational intelligence mirrors how human investigators think, linking clues across contexts but does so at speeds no person could match.

Predictive AI also supports **dynamic risk scoring**, allowing institutions to assign real-time risk levels to users or transactions. Instead of rigid categories, these systems continuously update scores based on behavior, geography, device trust, and even market sentiment. A user's risk score can change minute by minute, reflecting the dynamic nature of online finance. This approach reduces both false positives and false negatives, achieving a balance between vigilance and convenience. It also enables **tiered intervention**, where low-risk events are approved automatically while high-risk transactions trigger step-up authentication or manual review.

The implications of predictive modeling extend beyond fraud detection. They influence strategic decision-making, capital allocation, and policy formation. By understanding where risks are most likely to emerge, institutions can invest proactively rather than reactively. Regulators, too, benefit from these insights, using predictive analytics to forecast systemic vulnerabilities across the financial sector. Over time, predictive risk modeling could transform compliance from a rule-following exercise into a forward-looking discipline that anticipates crises before they reach the public.

However, predictive modeling also introduces new responsibilities. Forecasting risk means influencing behavior and with that comes ethical power. If models are biased or poorly calibrated, they may unfairly target specific demographics or market segments. Institutions must therefore ensure that predictive systems are transparent, auditable, and continuously refined. The goal is not simply to predict risk but to predict responsibly, aligning accuracy with fairness.

4.2 Ethical Frontiers of Automated Decision-Making

Artificial intelligence may excel at pattern recognition and prediction, but it operates within the ethical boundaries that humans define. As AI becomes more autonomous, capable of making decisions that directly affect people's financial lives, questions of ethics, accountability, and transparency grow more urgent. The frontier of automated decision-making is not merely technological; it is moral.

At its core, every AI-driven decision reflects an embedded set of values; whether consciously designed or unconsciously inherited from data. When an algorithm flags a transaction as suspicious, freezes an account, or denies a loan, it exerts real power over human livelihoods. The legitimacy of such power depends on **explainability**, the ability to show why the system acted the way it did. Yet, as AI models become more complex, their internal logic becomes less interpretable. Deep learning networks may involve thousands of parameters that even their creators cannot fully explain. This opacity threatens one of the cornerstones of financial regulation: accountability.

To address this challenge, the field of Explainable AI (XAI) has emerged as a moral and operational necessity. XAI seeks to bridge the gap between machine intelligence and human understanding by designing models that can articulate their reasoning in plain language. For instance, instead of simply labeling a transaction as "high risk," an explainable system might state, "This transaction was flagged because the device location differs from the user's recent login history, and the amount exceeds their average by 200 percent." Such transparency not only satisfies regulatory requirements but also builds trust among users who want to understand how decisions affecting them are made.

Ethical automation also demands human oversight, what regulators describe as a "human in the loop." Machines can analyze vast data sets, but they lack moral judgment. A decision that is statistically sound might still be socially unjust. Human review ensures that algorithms remain instruments of judgment, not replacements for it. In practice, this means designing workflows where human experts validate AI-driven outcomes, particularly in high-impact cases such as fraud claims, credit denial, or transaction blocking.

Another frontier of ethical concern is **data privacy**. AI systems feed on data, and their hunger for information often collides with the right to personal privacy. Financial institutions must walk a fine line between gathering enough data to make accurate predictions and respecting the boundaries of user consent. The rise in open banking and data-sharing initiatives has intensified this tension. Ethical AI governance requires strong data minimization principles, collecting only what is necessary, storing it securely, and deleting it responsibly. Moreover, institutions must ensure that anonymized data cannot be reverse-engineered to re-identify individuals, preserving trust in a world where data itself has become currency.

Equally significant is the challenge of **bias and discrimination**. Algorithms learn from history, and history contains inequality. Without intervention, AI systems can replicate patterns of exclusion embedded in past decisions. For example, if historical data associates' certain postal codes with higher fraud risk due to socioeconomic factors, the algorithm might unfairly penalize entire communities. Preventing such bias requires active ethical auditing, regular reviews of training data, diverse testing, and fairness metrics that measure equality of outcome. Some institutions now employ **AI ethics boards** to oversee these reviews, ensuring that automation enhances justice rather than undermines it.

As automation expands, the boundary between human and machine responsibility will continue to blur. When errors occur, accountability must remain clear. Institutions must establish governance models that define ownership of AI outcomes; from development to deployment. Documentation, traceability, and continuous evaluation should become as central to AI ethics as encryption is to cybersecurity. Only by doing so can financial institutions maintain public confidence in an era where algorithms increasingly act as unseen decision-makers.

In the end, the ethical frontier of AI in fraud detection is about balance between efficiency and empathy, automation and accountability. Technology can protect systems, but only ethics can protect trust. The most advanced algorithms are not those that detect the most fraud, but those that do so while upholding fairness, transparency, and respect for human dignity. Financial institutions that internalize this truth will lead the next generation of secure innovation, demonstrating that intelligence, whether artificial or human, reaches its highest form when guided by conscience.

CHAPTER FIVE

Blockchain, Transparency, and the Future of Secure Transactions

Trust is the currency of finance, and for centuries, trust has depended on intermediaries; banks, brokers, regulators, and auditors, institutions that verify authenticity and record ownership. Yet, every intermediary adds friction, cost, and vulnerability. The emergence of blockchain technology disrupted this century-old structure by proposing a radical question: What if trust could be built into the system itself? What if verification could occur automatically, without central authority, and with complete transparency? The answer to that question is reshaping global finance and redefining how cybersecurity is understood in the digital age.

Blockchain, often associated with cryptocurrencies, is far more than a tool for digital money. It is a distributed ledger technology that records transactions across multiple computers in such a way that no single participant controls the system, and every entry is verifiable by consensus. Once recorded, a transaction cannot be altered without altering all subsequent records, an act practically impossible without majority control of the network. In essence, blockchain replaces institutional trust with mathematical certainty. Its design ensures integrity, transparency, and immutability, making it one of the most secure data structures ever conceived.

The implications for financial security are profound. In traditional systems, a single breach at a central database can expose millions of records. In a blockchain, however, there is no central point of failure. Each participant holds a copy of the ledger, and consensus mechanisms such as Proof of Work (PoW) or Proof of Stake (PoS) validate every new transaction. This decentralization makes tampering exceedingly difficult. Cybercriminals cannot simply infiltrate one server; they would need to compromise the majority of nodes simultaneously, a feat both technically and economically unfeasible.

Beyond resilience, blockchain introduces transparency as a new dimension of security. Every transaction recorded on a public blockchain is visible to all participants, creating a permanent, auditable trail of activity. For regulators and auditors, this transparency offers a dream once thought impossible; real-time oversight. Financial institutions can trace the movement of assets, verify compliance, and detect irregularities instantly. The technology turns accountability from a procedural task into an embedded feature. It ensures that the integrity of records is no longer dependent on faith in intermediaries but guaranteed by the structure of the system itself.

However, blockchain's transparency also raises complex questions about privacy. While transaction data may be pseudonymous, patterns of activity can reveal identities when combined with external information. Financial institutions and regulators must therefore strike a delicate balance between openness and confidentiality. Solutions such as zero-knowledge proofs, which allow data verification without revealing the underlying information, represent a promising compromise. They make it possible to prove legitimacy while maintaining privacy, an essential requirement for compliance with regulations such as GDPR and NDPR.

The most transformative application of blockchain in finance lies in smart contracts; self-executing agreements coded directly into the blockchain. These contracts perform actions automatically when predefined conditions are met. For instance, an insurance payout could be triggered as soon as a verified event, such as flight cancellation, is recorded. In banking, smart contracts enable instant settlement of loans, trade finance, or asset transfers without the need for intermediaries. By automating trust, smart contracts reduce fraud risk, minimize disputes, and accelerate transaction speed. Yet, they also introduce a new category of risk: code vulnerability. A single flaw in contract logic can be exploited irreversibly, as transactions on blockchain cannot be rolled back. For this reason, secure coding practices and contract auditing have become indispensable components of blockchain cybersecurity.

The rise of decentralized finance (DeFi) has expanded blockchain's reach beyond institutional use to a borderless ecosystem of peer-to-peer financial services. DeFi platforms allow users to lend, borrow, trade, and earn interest without banks. They embody the democratization of finance, but also its volatility. While DeFi removes intermediaries, it transfers responsibility for security to the users and developers of the platform. Exploits in smart contracts, manipulated price oracles, and poorly designed protocols have led to billions in losses. These incidents underline a fundamental truth: decentralization may eliminate traditional gatekeepers, but it does not eliminate risk. It redistributes it.

From a regulatory perspective, blockchain presents both promise and paradox. On one hand, it enables greater transparency, auditability, and anti-money laundering (AML) capabilities. On the other, it challenges existing legal frameworks that depend on central authority. Regulators must now answer unprecedented questions: Who is accountable when a decentralized network fails? How can consumer protection be enforced when no entity controls the platform? These questions highlight the need for adaptive regulation; frameworks flexible enough to govern innovation without stifling it. Some jurisdictions have begun implementing regulatory sandboxes, where blockchain projects can operate under controlled conditions while policymakers observe their risks and benefits. This collaborative approach is gradually redefining the relationship between innovation and oversight.

Blockchain also reimagines identity and authentication in cybersecurity. Through decentralized digital identity (DDI) systems, individuals can control their credentials such as passports, academic records, or financial histories without relying on central repositories. These self-sovereign identities allow verification without disclosure, granting users autonomy over their data. For financial institutions, this could revolutionize Know Your Customer (KYC) processes. Instead of storing sensitive data themselves, they can validate transactions through blockchain-based attestations, reducing liability while maintaining compliance. The result is a model where security and privacy coexist rather than compete.

In the realm of payments and settlements, blockchain's efficiency is redefining speed and cost. Cross-border transfers that once took days now occur in minutes with minimal fees. Central banks worldwide are exploring Central Bank Digital Currencies (CBDCs); digital versions of national currencies built on blockchain or distributed ledger technologies. These currencies aim to combine the efficiency of digital payment systems with the stability of sovereign money. Yet, they also introduce new cybersecurity challenges: how to secure digital wallets, prevent double spending, and ensure resilience against systemic cyberattacks. The success of CBDCs will depend on achieving the right balance between control, transparency, and privacy, a balance still being negotiated on the global stage.

Despite its promise, blockchain is not a panacea. Its immutability, while a strength, can become a weakness when errors or illegal content are permanently recorded. Its decentralization, while resilient, can slow decision-making and complicate accountability. Moreover, its energy consumption; particularly in proof-of-work systems, raises sustainability concerns that cannot be ignored. As the world moves toward green finance and ESG compliance, blockchain must evolve toward more energy-efficient consensus mechanisms. Emerging models like Proof of Authority (PoA) and Proof of History (PoH) aim to address this by combining security with environmental responsibility.

The integration of blockchain into financial ecosystems represents a philosophical shift as much as a technical one. It redefines the nature of trust; transforming it from an institutionally conferred quality into a mathematically verifiable one. Yet even this new architecture of trust requires human stewardship. Technology can ensure transparency, but it cannot guarantee fairness. It can verify transactions, but it cannot enforce ethics. The responsibility to use blockchain wisely remains with the people and institutions that design, deploy, and regulate it.

The future of secure transactions will therefore depend on a hybrid model; one that combines the precision of decentralized technology with the accountability of human governance. Financial institutions will increasingly operate within interoperable ecosystems, where blockchains, AI systems, and regulatory frameworks communicate seamlessly. In this convergence lies the potential for a global financial network that is not only faster and safer but also more inclusive and transparent.

Blockchain is more than a technological revolution; it is a philosophical declaration, that transparency can coexist with privacy, that automation can coexist with ethics, and that trust can be engineered without losing its human essence. It offers finance a mirror in which to see both its progress and its principles. The challenge now is not to decide whether blockchain will shape the future of transactions, but how wisely humanity will shape the blockchain itself.

5.1 Blockchain in Compliance and Auditing

One of the most revolutionary yet underappreciated contributions of blockchain technology lies in its ability to transform compliance and auditing from reactive procedures into continuous, automated processes. Traditionally, financial audits involve periodic reviews conducted long after transactions occur. Auditors sift through records, validate balances, and cross-check documentation to ensure regulatory conformity. This retrospective approach, though thorough, is slow, expensive, and susceptible to human oversight. Blockchain, by contrast, embeds auditability directly into its structure. Every transaction is recorded immutably, time-stamped, and cryptographically linked to the one before it, creating a chain of evidence that cannot be altered or hidden.

For auditors, this means that verification no longer depends on trust in the data provided by an institution; it depends on mathematics. .Blockchain allows for **real-time auditing**, where compliance officers and regulators can observe transactions as they happen, ensuring continuous adherence to laws such as anti-money laundering (AML) and counter-terrorist financing (CTF) statutes. Smart contracts can even automate compliance functions by enforcing rules within the transaction itself. For instance, a cross-border payment smart contract could be programmed to verify that both sender and receiver identities are authenticated under KYC standards before execution.

The potential for fraud or error is drastically reduced when compliance becomes an inherent feature of the system rather than an afterthought. This form of regtech integration, where regulatory technology operates alongside blockchain infrastructure, represents the next phase in financial governance. Regulators, however, must adapt their oversight models to this new transparency. The challenge will not be in accessing information but in interpreting and contextualizing it. As blockchain enables a flood of real-time data, institutions will need AI-powered tools to analyze compliance signals and detect anomalies at scale. In the future, the line between auditing and cybersecurity will blur, as both rely on the same immutable record of truth.

5.2 Environmental and Ethical Implications of Distributed Finance

As transformative as blockchain is, it does not exist in a vacuum. Every transaction on a distributed ledger consumes energy, and every innovation carries ethical implications. Early blockchain systems, especially those using Proof of Work (PoW) consensus, were notoriously energy-intensive. Mining cryptocurrencies required immense computational power, leading to concerns about carbon emissions and environmental sustainability. Critics argued that the energy used to secure digital assets could power entire nations. While newer models such as Proof of Stake (PoS) have reduced energy consumption drastically, the ethical debate surrounding blockchain's ecological footprint remains unresolved.

Financial institutions integrating blockchain into their operations must now consider not just technological efficiency but environmental responsibility. Green finance initiatives and ESG (Environmental, Social, and Governance) frameworks increasingly require transparency about the sustainability of digital infrastructure. The same transparency that secures financial trust must now secure ecological trust. Institutions are responding by exploring **carbon-neutral blockchains** that offset emissions through renewable energy credits and by supporting blockchain networks that use energy-efficient algorithms.

The ethics of distributed finance extend beyond the environment. Blockchain democratizes access to financial systems, giving unbanked populations tools for saving, trading, and investing. Yet, it can also amplify inequality when adoption is concentrated among the technologically privileged. True ethical progress requires inclusion, designing blockchain interfaces and literacy programs that make participation accessible across socioeconomic boundaries. Ethical blockchain governance must ensure that transparency does not become surveillance and that decentralization does not devolve into disorder.

Moreover, as digital assets proliferate, questions of moral ownership arise. Who bears responsibility when decentralized systems facilitate illicit activity, the coder, the platform, or the collective network? Ethical finance in the age of blockchain demands accountability mechanisms that match its scale of innovation. It must align with human values of fairness, sustainability, and justice, ensuring that the pursuit of transparency does not overshadow compassion.

5.3 Interoperability and the Path to Global Financial Integration

For blockchain to achieve its full transformative potential, it must transcend its current fragmentation. Today's blockchain ecosystem resembles a constellation of isolated islands, each with its own rules, standards, and currencies. Public, private, and consortium blockchains coexist but rarely communicate. This lack of interoperability limits scalability and efficiency. A transaction validated on one blockchain often cannot be recognized on another, hindering the seamless movement of assets across systems. True global financial integration will depend on bridging these divides.

Interoperability; the ability of different blockchain networks to exchange information and assets, represents the next frontier of digital finance. Projects such as Polkadot, Cosmos, and Hyperledger Cactus are pioneering frameworks that allow blockchains to communicate through standardized protocols. For financial institutions, interoperability promises a unified infrastructure where assets can move freely between networks without losing traceability or security. Imagine a future where a remittance initiated on one blockchain can be settled instantly on another, with regulators able to monitor both in real time.

Interoperability will also accelerate the convergence of traditional finance (TradFi) and decentralized finance (DeFi). Central banks, commercial banks, fintech startups, and crypto networks will eventually operate within a shared digital ecosystem. This fusion could enable unprecedented efficiency, but it also raises regulatory and security questions. How do we enforce compliance in a system that spans jurisdictions and governance models? The answer will lie in standardized digital governance frameworks, where global institutions agree on shared rules for data privacy, smart contract auditing, and cyber resilience.

Technologically, interoperability may evolve through cross-chain bridges and layer-two protocols that enable scalability while maintaining consensus security. However, these bridges themselves must be fortified, as they have become targets of sophisticated cyberattacks. The pursuit of global integration must therefore proceed hand in hand with the pursuit of security, an equilibrium that requires cooperation among engineers, regulators, and policymakers.

Philosophically, interoperability represents more than connectivity; it symbolizes unity. It envisions a financial world where transparency, accountability, and inclusion are not regional privileges but universal rights. Blockchain, when made interoperable, can serve as the backbone of a truly global economy, one where the barriers of trust, geography, and bureaucracy dissolve into a single, shared ledger of truth.

CHAPTER SIX

Building Cyber Resilience in Financial Institutions

The true measure of a financial institution's strength is not the absence of attacks but the ability to endure and recover from them. In an era when cyber threats evolve faster than regulations, and digital operations extend beyond physical boundaries, resilience has become the defining quality of survival. Cyber resilience is more than cybersecurity. It is a philosophy that integrates protection, adaptation, and recovery into the fabric of financial systems. Where cybersecurity focuses on prevention, cyber resilience focuses on continuity. It ensures that even when systems are compromised, trust and functionality remain intact.

In the financial sector, resilience is both a technical and human discipline. It encompasses not only encrypted firewalls and backup systems but also leadership foresight, organizational culture, and decision-making under pressure. A resilient bank, payment processor, or fintech company is one that anticipates disruption and prepares to operate through it. This preparation requires the fusion of strategy, governance, and technology into a continuous cycle of improvement.

The foundation of resilience begins with **risk awareness**. Financial institutions must understand their threat landscape before they can build defenses that withstand it. This involves mapping critical assets, identifying vulnerabilities, and assessing the potential impact of each threat scenario. Unlike static risk assessment models, modern frameworks are dynamic and iterative. They evolve as new technologies, regulations, and attack patterns emerge. Scenario-based planning is an essential part of this process. Institutions simulate real-world incidents, such as ransomware infiltration or insider breaches, to evaluate their capacity for response and recovery. These exercises reveal weak points in communication, decision-making, and technical infrastructure that cannot be detected through audits alone.

Beyond awareness, resilience depends on **redundancy and diversity**. A single point of failure can bring an entire financial system to a halt. To prevent this, institutions adopt layered defenses and alternative systems. Data replication across multiple secure locations, backup power sources, and secondary communication channels ensure continuity even under attack. Diversity also applies to technology providers. Overreliance on a single vendor or cloud service creates hidden dependencies that can amplify disruption. By diversifying infrastructure and suppliers, institutions distribute risk across a wider surface, reducing vulnerability.

A central pillar of resilience is **incident response readiness**. The best-prepared organizations assume that breaches will occur and plan accordingly. A comprehensive incident response plan defines clear roles, escalation paths, and decision protocols for different types of cyber events. The plan must be regularly tested, updated, and integrated into daily operations. It should not exist as a document on a shelf but as a living system practiced by all departments. Communication is key. During a crisis, transparency between technical teams, executives, regulators, and customers is as important as containment. Silence breeds speculation, while timely updates preserve trust. The ability to manage both technical and reputational aspects of a breach defines true institutional maturity.

Technology alone cannot ensure resilience without **human capacity and culture**. The people within a financial institution form its first and last line of defense. Building resilience requires training employees not just to follow procedures but to think critically in uncertain situations. Cyber awareness programs should go beyond phishing simulations to include adaptive problem-solving and crisis behavior. A culture that encourages accountability and learning, rather than blame, empowers staff to report anomalies early. In resilient organizations, mistakes become lessons, and lessons become policies. This feedback loop transforms cybersecurity from a set of controls into an evolving mindset shared by everyone.

Leadership plays a decisive role in shaping this mindset. Boards and executives must view cyber resilience as a strategic imperative, not an operational afterthought. Investment in resilience should be seen as investment in reputation and stability. The most forward-looking institutions appoint Chief Resilience Officers or integrate resilience oversight into existing governance frameworks. This ensures that technology budgets, risk management priorities, and compliance objectives align with the institution's resilience goals. Leadership must also model composure during crises. When executives communicate calmly, make evidence-based decisions, and maintain ethical transparency, they set the tone for the entire organization's response.

Modern resilience strategies increasingly rely on **automation and intelligence**. Artificial intelligence can detect anomalies faster than human analysts, predicting potential failures and automatically initiating containment protocols. Machine learning systems can correlate thousands of signals, identifying early indicators of compromise. Automation ensures that critical actions, such as isolating infected networks or activating data recovery processes, occur instantly without waiting for manual input. However, automation must be designed with oversight. Blind reliance on algorithms can introduce new risks, especially if systems act on incomplete or misleading data. Combining automation with human review achieves both speed and judgment.

An emerging frontier of cyber resilience is collaborative defense. In the interconnected financial ecosystem, no institution operates in isolation. A breach in one entity can cascade through payment networks, supply chains, and interbank systems. Collaborative defense involves sharing threat intelligence, attack indicators, and recovery insights across the industry. Many countries now operate Financial Sector Computer Emergency Response Teams (FinCERTs) or industry-specific resilience forums that coordinate defense efforts. By pooling knowledge, institutions transform isolated vulnerabilities into collective strength. This spirit of cooperation represents a shift from secrecy to solidarity, acknowledging that resilience is a shared responsibility.

Resilience also depends on regulatory alignment. Regulators around the world increasingly require financial institutions to demonstrate operational resilience alongside cybersecurity compliance. Frameworks such as the Bank of England's Operational Resilience Policy, the European Union's Digital Operational Resilience Act, and Nigeria's Risk-Based Cybersecurity Framework emphasize business continuity, incident reporting, and recovery capability. These policies reflect a new understanding that resilience is not optional but integral to systemic stability. Institutions that fail to invest in it risk not only financial penalties but loss of public confidence.

At the technical level, resilience is reinforced through **business continuity management**. This includes maintaining secure backups, redundant data centers, and tested recovery procedures. Backup systems must be isolated from primary networks to prevent simultaneous compromise during ransomware attacks. Recovery testing is equally vital. Institutions that never test their backups often discover too late that data cannot be restored. Regular drills, combined with independent assessments, validate readiness and reveal hidden dependencies.

Resilience extends beyond technology and governance into **psychological readiness**. Crises exert immense pressure on employees, demanding fast and accurate decisions under stress. Institutions that invest in mental preparedness, team coordination, and leadership training recover more effectively. Psychological resilience also applies to customers and partners. Clear communication, empathy, and visible competence during disruptions can turn potential panic into patience. The ability to maintain composure and trust in the midst of uncertainty distinguishes institutions that survive crises from those that collapse under them.

As threats evolve, resilience must evolve too. The future of cyber resilience will be defined by adaptability. Emerging technologies such as quantum computing, 5G networks, and decentralized systems will reshape both the risk landscape and the tools available to defend it. Financial institutions must adopt adaptive resilience models, which treat every incident as data for improvement. Post-incident analysis should focus not only on technical causes but on systemic lessons, how governance, training, and design can be refined. In this way, resilience becomes a continuous cycle of anticipation, absorption, recovery, and transformation.

At its heart, resilience is an expression of humility. It acknowledges that no system is invincible and no defense permanent. It accepts that failure is inevitable but insists that recovery is possible. The institutions that embody this philosophy become stronger with every test. They move from fearing uncertainty to mastering it. Cyber resilience is not merely a strategy for defense; it is a discipline for endurance. It ensures that when the next wave of disruption arrives and it will, the systems that guard global finance will bend, but never break.

6.1 Psychological and Organizational Resilience

Cyber resilience begins with infrastructure but is sustained by people. Financial institutions often invest millions in firewalls, encryption, and recovery systems yet overlook the psychological and organizational factors that determine how effectively those systems perform during crises. Resilience at the human level means more than technical competence; it means emotional stability, clear thinking, and trust in leadership under pressure. When a cyber incident occurs, panic can spread faster than malware. People freeze, make reactive decisions, or hesitate to report mistakes. The ability of an organization to withstand and recover from digital disruption therefore depends on the collective composure and coordination of its workforce.

Psychological resilience starts with awareness and preparedness. Employees must understand not only what to do during an attack but why their actions matter. Regular simulations and crisis exercises train the mind to respond instinctively rather than emotionally. These exercises should include not only technical staff but executives, public relations officers, and customer service teams. A unified sense of responsibility strengthens confidence. When staff believe they are part of a capable and transparent system, their response becomes swift and coordinated.

Beyond preparedness, institutions must cultivate a **learning culture**. Mistakes are inevitable, but the response to them determines growth. A punitive environment discourages disclosure, allowing small errors to escalate into major incidents. A learning culture encourages honesty, reflection, and systemic improvement. Post-incident reviews should focus on insight rather than blame. Psychological resilience also includes caring for employee wellbeing after crises. The mental fatigue that follows prolonged cyberattacks can lead to burnout and decreased vigilance. Providing support, recognition, and recovery time ensures that resilience is sustainable.

Leadership behavior sets the tone for organizational resilience. Calm, consistent communication during disruptions prevents confusion and rumors. When executives share verified updates, acknowledge challenges, and show empathy, they reinforce trust both internally and externally. Institutions that integrate psychological training into their crisis management frameworks not only recover faster but also emerge stronger. In the long term, human resilience becomes the most stable foundation of all technological resilience.

6.2 Collaborative Industry Defense and Shared Intelligence

In a globalized financial system, no organization is isolated. Cyber threats travel through interconnected networks, shared service providers, and third-party infrastructures. A breach in one institution can quickly cascade across others. This interdependence demands a new model of protection; one based on collaboration rather than competition. **Collaborative defense** transforms cybersecurity from a private battle into a collective mission.

Shared intelligence is the cornerstone of this collaboration. When institutions exchange information about threats, vulnerabilities, and attack techniques, they shorten the learning curve for the entire industry. Financial Sector Computer Emergency Response Teams (FinCERTs), Information Sharing and Analysis Centers (ISACs), and industry coalitions already facilitate this process across regions. These platforms collect, anonymize, and distribute actionable threat intelligence, enabling faster identification and containment of attacks. In some cases, regulators also participate, bridging public oversight with private expertise.

The benefits of collaboration extend beyond defense. Joint training programs, shared simulations, and coordinated incident response exercises build trust between institutions. Competitors in the marketplace become allies in resilience. This unity reduces duplication of effort and improves overall response speed during large-scale attacks. Shared intelligence also enhances **situational awareness** at the national and international levels. When banks and fintechs report incidents promptly, authorities can detect patterns of coordinated cybercrime and mobilize countermeasures before damage spreads.

However, collaborative defense requires trust. Institutions must share enough information to be useful without exposing sensitive data that could create new risks. This balance is achieved through legal frameworks and data-sharing protocols that ensure confidentiality while promoting transparency. Advanced encryption, anonymization, and blockchain-based data exchange platforms are making secure collaboration more feasible.

Collaboration also extends to the supply chain. Vendors, cloud service providers, and payment processors must be integrated into the same defense ecosystem. Third-party risk management evolves into **ecosystem risk management**, recognizing that resilience depends on the collective health of all connected partners. In the future, collaborative defense will define financial cybersecurity maturity. It reflects the reality that in a networked world, survival is not individual but shared.

6.3 Adaptive Resilience in the Age of Quantum Threats

The next great test of cyber resilience will come from quantum computing. While quantum technology promises breakthroughs in data analysis, modeling, and computation, it also poses unprecedented risks to encryption; the very foundation of digital security. Current cryptographic systems, such as RSA and elliptic curve encryption, rely on the computational difficulty of factoring large prime numbers. Quantum computers, using quantum bits and parallel computation, could solve these problems exponentially faster, rendering much of today's encryption obsolete.

For financial institutions, this represents a paradigm shift. The systems that currently protect global payments, digital identities, and blockchain networks could be compromised once quantum technology reaches maturity. Preparing for this era requires **adaptive resilience** — the ability to anticipate disruption before it materializes. Institutions must begin transitioning toward **post-quantum cryptography**, which employs algorithms designed to withstand quantum attacks. This migration is complex, as it involves upgrading software, hardware, and operational processes across entire ecosystems. Yet early adoption will distinguish leaders from laggards in the new security landscape.

Adaptive resilience also demands **continuous innovation**. Institutions must treat resilience not as a static goal but as an evolving discipline. Artificial intelligence can help by predicting where vulnerabilities may emerge once quantum systems are commercialized. Partnerships with research institutions and technology firms will be essential for staying ahead of advancements. Governments and central banks must also play a role by defining national quantum security standards and fostering collaboration between public and private sectors.

Beyond encryption, quantum computing may redefine resilience through its capacity to model complex cyberattack scenarios and simulate system responses in real time. Institutions could use quantum-powered analytics to test the limits of their defenses and optimize recovery strategies with unmatched precision. However, this same power in malicious hands could amplify threats to a level unseen before. Adaptive resilience will therefore rely on foresight, cooperation, and regulation working together to balance innovation with security.

The transition to the quantum era will not happen overnight, but preparation must begin now. The institutions that build adaptive frameworks; frameworks that evolve with technology rather than react to it will not only survive future disruptions but shape them. In doing so, they will redefine resilience for the century ahead, proving that readiness is not about predicting every threat but about remaining strong amid every change.

CHAPTER SEVEN

The Human Factor in Financial Cybersecurity

Technology may power the financial world, but it is people who make it work. Every system, from high-frequency trading platforms to digital banking networks, ultimately depends on human decisions. Cybersecurity, therefore, is not just a technical science but a human discipline. It is shaped by the choices, habits, and values of those who build, manage, and use technology. No matter how advanced a defense system is, one careless click, one weak password, or one ignored alert can compromise it entirely. The human factor remains the most unpredictable and decisive element in the security chain.

Understanding the human element in financial cybersecurity requires looking beyond error to psychology, behavior, and culture. People do not make mistakes simply because they are uninformed. They act under pressure, fatigue, or misplaced confidence. Financial environments are fast-paced, where efficiency and results are often prioritized over caution. Employees are expected to process thousands of digital interactions daily. In such conditions, security can easily become a background task rather than a conscious priority. Building resilience around this reality means creating systems and cultures that support good decisions, even when circumstances are stressful.

The first layer of human-centered cybersecurity lies in awareness and education. Training programs should go beyond technical guidelines to address behavioral patterns. Employees must learn to recognize manipulation tactics used by social engineers who exploit trust and authority. Cyber awareness must be constant, not periodic. Workshops, phishing simulations, and real-time feedback keep vigilance sharp. However, training alone is not enough. It must be supported by reinforcement mechanisms that make secure behavior easy and natural. Password managers, automated access controls, and secure communication tools reduce the burden on users, ensuring compliance without frustration.

Financial institutions must also understand the psychology of risk perception. Humans tend to underestimate risks that are abstract and overestimate those that are visible. Cyber threats are often invisible until damage occurs, which makes them psychologically distant. To bridge this gap, organizations should use storytelling and scenario-based learning that bring risks to life. When employees see how a single phishing email led to millions in losses for another firm, the lesson becomes real. Risk communication should appeal to both logic and emotion, balancing data with narrative to cultivate genuine vigilance.

Leadership plays a critical role in defining how people perceive security. When executives demonstrate that cybersecurity is a shared priority, it becomes embedded in the organization's culture. A Chief Information Security Officer who collaborates with business leaders rather than issuing directives from isolation fosters unity. Security messages from top management should be clear, consistent, and aligned with the company's mission. Employees are more likely to follow rules when they see leaders modeling the same behavior.

Trust is another cornerstone of the human factor. Paradoxically, both too much and too little trust can weaken security. Excessive trust leads to complacency; insufficient trust leads to inefficiency. The key is balanced trust supported by verification. The principle of zero trust, where every access request is verified regardless of its origin, reflects this philosophy. Yet even within that framework, human relationships matter. Teams must trust that security processes exist to protect, not to punish. Transparency about why certain protocols are enforced reduces resistance and builds cooperation.

Insider threats represent one of the most complex challenges in financial cybersecurity. Insiders include employees, contractors, or partners who misuse their legitimate access for malicious or careless purposes. They have the keys to the system, which makes their actions harder to detect. Some insiders act out of greed or revenge, while others are manipulated through coercion or personal vulnerability. Preventing insider breaches requires both technical and emotional intelligence. Monitoring systems can track unusual activity, but human engagement identifies warning signs such as sudden behavioral changes or declining morale. Institutions that promote employee wellbeing, fair treatment, and ethical accountability reduce the likelihood of internal sabotage.

The human factor extends beyond employees to customers. Financial cybersecurity depends on public behavior as much as institutional defense. Many cyberattacks exploit customers through fake investment schemes, fraudulent emails, or malicious mobile apps. Educating customers about digital hygiene, scam identification, and safe transaction practices should be part of every financial organization's outreach. The tone of such education matters. Customers respond better to empowerment than to fear. When institutions position security as a shared responsibility rather than a technical barrier, users become partners in defense.

Emotional intelligence plays an underappreciated role in cybersecurity management. Analysts, engineers, and response teams operate in high-stress environments where decisions have immediate consequences. Fatigue, frustration, and burnout can impair judgment. Institutions must cultivate empathy within leadership structures, ensuring that employees feel valued and supported. Regular rotations, mental health programs, and transparent communication reduce stress and sustain motivation. A resilient workforce is not only skilled but emotionally stable.

Culture remains the strongest predictor of long-term cybersecurity success. An organization's culture defines how people respond when rules conflict with convenience, when deadlines clash with caution, and when crises strike without warning. A culture of accountability encourages employees to report mistakes early, while a culture of fear hides them until they escalate. Encouraging curiosity and open discussion turns cybersecurity into a shared pursuit of improvement rather than a checklist of compliance. The tone of culture is set from the top but sustained from the bottom. Every employee, regardless of role, contributes to it through daily choices.

Behavioral science is increasingly being used to design systems that align with human tendencies. Instead of expecting perfect discipline, security architects now apply human-centered design principles to minimize opportunities for error. Interfaces that provide clear prompts, systems that guide users through secure workflows, and alerts that explain context instead of overwhelming users all contribute to better outcomes. In cybersecurity, the best defense is not the most complex system but the one that people can and will use correctly.

The relationship between humans and technology is evolving rapidly with the rise of automation and artificial intelligence. As machines take on more security functions, the role of humans shifts from execution to supervision. This transition introduces new challenges of trust and accountability. People must trust machines to act correctly, while machines depend on people for ethical guidance. This interdependence demands a new kind of literacy — one that blends technical understanding with moral clarity. The institutions that cultivate this literacy will navigate the future of cybersecurity with confidence and responsibility.

In the end, the human factor in financial cybersecurity is both the greatest risk and the greatest asset. People create vulnerabilities, but they also create solutions. They write the code, interpret the data, and make the decisions that determine whether technology serves stability or chaos. The goal is not to eliminate human error but to empower human strength. When institutions invest equally in people and technology, they build systems that can adapt, learn, and recover. The future of financial cybersecurity will not be decided by machines alone, but by the wisdom, discipline, and empathy of the people who guide them.

7.1 Behavioral Engineering and Secure Design

One of the most transformative ideas in modern cybersecurity is that people do not fail because they are careless, but because systems are not designed to support natural human behavior. Behavioral engineering applies insights from psychology, design, and data science to create security processes that align with how people think and act. In financial systems, where thousands of decisions are made every second, simplicity can be a stronger defense than sophistication.

Traditional cybersecurity assumes that users should adapt to technology. Behavioral engineering reverses this logic by adapting technology to users. Password policies that require complex combinations of symbols and numbers often lead to weaker practices such as writing them down or reusing them. Behavioral design replaces such friction with solutions like biometric authentication and password less logins that enhance both convenience and protection. Similarly, security alerts designed with empathy rather than alarmism encourage engagement instead of avoidance.

Human-centered design also reduces cognitive overload, the state where too many instructions or warnings cause users to ignore them altogether. Financial interfaces cluttered with confusing messages can push even well-intentioned employees to bypass security controls. The goal of secure design is not to add more steps but to make the right steps effortless. For example, two-factor authentication systems that integrate smoothly with mobile devices experience higher adoption than those requiring separate hardware tokens. When security becomes intuitive, compliance follows naturally.

Behavioral engineering is especially powerful when combined with analytics. Institutions can study user behavior patterns to identify where security friction occurs and redesign those touchpoints for better engagement. Data on how employees interact with authentication systems, email filters, or digital forms helps tailor training and tools to their needs. This continuous loop of observation, feedback, and refinement turns security into an adaptive ecosystem rather than a rigid framework. In the long run, the best cybersecurity systems are those that make safe behavior the easiest option.

7.2 Leadership and Ethical Culture in Security

No institution can rise above the values of its leadership. In cybersecurity, ethics and culture begin at the top. When executives treat security as a cost center or a regulatory burden, that perception spreads through the organization. When they frame it as an expression of integrity and trust, it becomes a shared mission. Leadership shapes not only strategy but morale. It signals whether people should act out of fear of punishment or pride in protection.

An ethical cybersecurity culture depends on **clarity and consistency**. Employees must know that ethical behavior will be supported, even when it exposes flaws or mistakes. A staff member who reports a vulnerability should be rewarded for responsibility, not reprimanded for inconvenience. This encourages openness and accelerates learning. Ethical cultures thrive on transparency, and transparency thrives on trust.

Leadership also involves modeling humility. Even the most advanced organizations are not immune to breaches, and pretending otherwise breeds denial. Executives who acknowledge risks openly and invest in realistic contingency planning set a powerful precedent. They communicate that security is a shared responsibility, not a departmental function. Regular briefings, board-level oversight, and integration of cybersecurity metrics into performance evaluation make security a visible priority.

Ethical culture extends to partnerships and public communication. When institutions are transparent about incidents, they preserve credibility even in crisis. Concealment may protect reputation momentarily but erodes trust in the long term. Ethical leadership transforms setbacks into opportunities for improvement and public education. It demonstrates that integrity is measured not by perfection but by accountability. Financial institutions that lead with this mindset do more than secure their systems; they elevate the moral standard of the industry itself.

7.3 Customer Awareness and Digital Trust

In the digital economy, customers are no longer passive users but active participants in security. Every login, payment, or data disclosure contributes to the overall health of financial ecosystems. Yet, many customers underestimate their role or feel overwhelmed by technical jargon. Building digital trust begins with empowerment; giving customers the knowledge and tools to protect themselves confidently.

Financial institutions must invest in clear communication that demystifies security. Terms such as encryption, phishing, or tokenization should be explained in accessible language through websites, mobile apps, and marketing materials. When customers understand how systems protect them, they become more vigilant and cooperative. Awareness campaigns that use real-world examples of fraud prevention foster engagement more effectively than abstract warnings.

Digital trust also depends on transparency. Customers should know how their data is collected, stored, and shared. Privacy policies written in legal language discourage understanding. Simplified, visual formats communicate respect for users and build credibility. Trust deepens when institutions allow customers to control their data preferences, such as opting in or out of marketing access or deciding which third-party integrations are permitted. Empowerment, in this sense, is both an ethical obligation and a security measure.

The rise of mobile banking and digital wallets has created new opportunities and new risks. Fraudsters now target customers through cloned websites, fake apps, and impersonation schemes. Educating users about digital verification such as checking app authenticity, validating URLs, and avoiding unsolicited links; prevents many of these attacks. Institutions can reinforce this awareness through push notifications, in-app tips, and guided onboarding processes.

Finally, digital trust is built on reliability. Customers must feel that systems work consistently and that institutions respond promptly when issues arise. Fast recovery, clear communication, and respectful handling of complaints strengthen long-term loyalty. Financial institutions that make customers feel safe do not just prevent breaches; they create advocates for security. Trust, once earned through transparency and reliability, becomes the strongest defense of all.

CHAPTER EIGHT

Cloud Security and Financial Infrastructure

The cloud has transformed the way financial institutions operate. What was once confined to physical servers and data centers has expanded into vast digital ecosystems that stretch across continents. Banks, fintech startups, and payment processors now rely on cloud platforms to store data, process transactions, and deliver services at unmatched speed and scale. The cloud has made finance more agile, more connected, and more intelligent. Yet, this very fluidity has also redrawn the boundaries of security. Protecting a cloud-based infrastructure demands a reimagining of how trust, control, and resilience are defined in the digital age.

At its core, the cloud represents a shift from ownership to access. Instead of maintaining local servers, financial institutions rent computing power and storage from third-party providers. This model allows them to scale rapidly, reduce costs, and focus on innovation. However, it also means that critical data and processes now reside on systems not entirely under their control. Security in the cloud is not a one-sided responsibility. It is a shared partnership between the provider and the customer, where each must understand and fulfill their part of the obligation.

The **shared responsibility model** is the foundation of cloud security. Cloud service providers secure the underlying infrastructure — the servers, networking, and physical data centers. Financial institutions, on the other hand, are responsible for securing their data, applications, and user access. The line between the two can blur, especially when multiple vendors and service layers are involved. Misconfigurations, weak access controls, and unmonitored third-party integrations often become the entry points for breaches. Clarity and accountability are therefore critical. Every institution using cloud services must define security ownership in detail and verify compliance through regular audits.

Encryption remains the most effective safeguard for data in the cloud. Financial data should be encrypted not only during transmission but also at rest. End-to-end encryption ensures that even if data is intercepted, it remains unreadable without authorized keys. Yet encryption alone is not enough. Key management practices must be robust and independent. Storing encryption keys on the same cloud environment as the data they protect undermines their purpose. Many institutions now use hardware security modules or external key management systems to maintain separation of control.

Access management is another cornerstone of cloud security. Financial institutions must operate on the principle of **least privilege**, granting users only the permissions necessary for their roles. Role-based access control prevents unnecessary exposure and limits the potential impact of compromised credentials. Multi-factor authentication adds a second layer of defense, ensuring that even stolen passwords cannot easily grant unauthorized access. The rise of identity and access management (IAM) platforms has made it possible to automate these controls across complex hybrid environments.

Cloud environments are dynamic, with resources constantly being created, modified, and removed. Static security models cannot keep up. Continuous monitoring through **cloud security posture management** (CSPM) tools allows institutions to detect misconfigurations, suspicious activity, and compliance violations in real time. Artificial intelligence enhances this process by learning normal patterns of behavior and flagging anomalies that may indicate intrusion or misuse. The ability to respond immediately to potential threats transforms security from a passive shield into an active defense mechanism.

Financial regulators have adapted to the growing dependence on cloud technology. Many now require institutions to conduct third-party risk assessments before engaging with cloud providers. These assessments evaluate not only technical standards but also legal and geographic factors. Data sovereignty; the requirement that certain types of data remain within national borders is one of the most complex issues in global cloud computing. Institutions operating across jurisdictions must ensure that their providers comply with local data protection laws, such as the EU's GDPR or Nigeria's NDPR.

While public clouds dominate financial innovation, many institutions adopt hybrid or multi-cloud strategies to balance flexibility with control. Hybrid models combine private infrastructure for sensitive workloads with public clouds for scalability. Multi-cloud approaches distribute operations across several providers to avoid dependency on one vendor. These strategies enhance resilience but also introduce complexity. Consistent security policies must be enforced across all environments to prevent gaps that attackers can exploit. Unified dashboards, centralized logging, and standardized configurations make it possible to maintain coherence across diverse infrastructures.

Resilience in the cloud depends heavily on **backup and recovery planning**. Cloud services offer high availability, but outages still occur. Financial institutions must design architectures that ensure business continuity even when a cloud region goes offline. Data replication across regions and automated failover systems are standard practices. However, recovery plans must also consider scenarios where access to the provider itself is disrupted, such as geopolitical restrictions or supply chain failures. True resilience means maintaining independence within interdependence; the ability to operate temporarily outside the provider's domain if necessary.

Another growing concern is supplying chain risk. The cloud is built upon layers of interconnected services, from infrastructure providers to application vendors and open-source components. A vulnerability in one layer can cascade through the entire chain. The SolarWinds incident of 2020 revealed how attackers can compromise trusted software updates to infiltrate networks undetected. Financial institutions must therefore perform continuous due diligence not only on their direct providers but on their providers' partners as well. Transparency and contractual clarity across the supply chain are essential for preventing hidden risks.

Compliance in the cloud era has evolved from static audits to continuous assurance. Regulatory frameworks such as ISO 27017 for cloud security and ISO 27018 for data privacy provide guidelines for cloud-specific controls. Financial institutions must document how their configurations align with these standards and maintain verifiable logs of security events. Automation tools now make it possible to generate compliance reports in real time, reducing manual effort and increasing reliability. The convergence of cybersecurity, compliance, and governance within the cloud is creating a new paradigm known as security as a service, where trust itself becomes an operational layer.

The final dimension of cloud security lies in human oversight and ethical accountability. While automation and artificial intelligence manage most of the operational tasks, humans remain responsible for defining ethical boundaries. Who monitors the monitors? Who ensures that automated defenses respect privacy while enforcing protection? Institutions must establish oversight committees that include cybersecurity experts, ethicists, and compliance officers to guide responsible use of cloud technologies. Ethical oversight ensures that efficiency never overrides the rights and dignity of those whose data is stored in the system.

The future of financial infrastructure will be defined by the seamless integration of cloud security, resilience, and ethics. Cloud technology is not a risk to be avoided but a tool to be mastered. It enables financial institutions to expand access, innovate faster, and serve customers globally. Yet, mastery requires humility; the awareness that technology magnifies both strengths and vulnerabilities. Institutions that understand this duality will lead the next phase of secure financial transformation. They will build infrastructures that are not only intelligent but trustworthy, not only connected but controlled, and not only digital but deeply human in design and purpose.

8.1 Shared Responsibility and Data Sovereignty

The promise of cloud computing rests on shared efficiency, but its reality depends on shared responsibility. Every financial institution that adopts cloud infrastructure must understand precisely where its duties begin and where the provider's end. The shared responsibility model, while conceptually simple, often becomes a source of misunderstanding in practice. Cloud providers secure the foundational layers; the hardware, networking, and physical environment but institutions remain accountable for protecting their applications, data, and user access. Misinterpretation of this boundary has been at the root of many data breaches in the financial industry.

The shared responsibility model also extends into governance. Institutions must conduct regular audits, implement encryption, and establish access controls. Providers, in turn, must ensure transparency about their internal controls, incident response processes, and data-handling practices. Effective governance is built on verification, not assumption. Many institutions now require Service Organization Control (SOC) reports, ISO 27001 certifications, and compliance attestations before onboarding any cloud provider. These certifications provide assurance that providers meet the same standards expected of financial institutions themselves.

Data sovereignty adds another layer of complexity. Every country has unique laws governing how financial and personal data can be stored or transferred. For multinational banks, a single customer record may pass through servers in multiple jurisdictions, each with different compliance rules. Regulations such as the European Union's General Data Protection Regulation (GDPR) and Nigeria's Data Protection Regulation (NDPR) mandate strict conditions for data export and user consent. Failure to comply can result in severe legal and financial penalties.

To navigate this landscape, financial institutions are adopting **geo-fencing strategies** that ensure sensitive data remains within approved regions. Cloud providers have responded by offering localized data centers that comply with regional laws. Still, ultimate accountability lies with the institution, not the provider. True compliance requires visibility into where data is processed and stored at all times. Data classification systems, encryption with geographically distributed keys, and legal audits form the pillars of a mature sovereignty strategy.

Shared responsibility and data sovereignty together represent the moral and operational backbone of cloud security. They define not only how institutions interact with technology but how they demonstrate accountability to customers, regulators, and the public. In the digital age, responsibility cannot be outsourced. It must be embedded in every transaction, every architecture, and every decision.

8.2 Automation and Continuous Compliance

Automation has become the lifeblood of cloud operations, allowing financial institutions to maintain security and compliance in environments that evolve by the minute. Unlike traditional data centers, where configurations remain relatively static, cloud systems are fluid. Servers spin up and down automatically, containers are deployed on demand, and applications update themselves without human intervention. In such conditions, manual oversight is insufficient. Continuous compliance; the real-time monitoring and enforcement of regulatory standards is essential.

Automation enables this continuous assurance. Security tools now integrate directly with cloud platforms to monitor configurations, permissions, and data flows. They detect violations instantly and, in many cases, correct them automatically. For instance, if a database becomes publicly exposed, automated systems can restrict access within seconds while alerting administrators. This combination of speed and precision minimizes exposure and ensures consistent adherence to policies.

Artificial intelligence enhances automation further by learning from historical data. Machine learning algorithms identify recurring compliance patterns, detect anomalies, and predict future vulnerabilities. For example, if a misconfiguration tends to occur during specific deployment cycles, predictive analytics can flag the risk before it reappears. Automation thus evolves from a reactive function into a preventive discipline.

Continuous compliance is particularly valuable in regulated sectors like finance, where audits are frequent and rigorous. Traditional audits rely on static evidence, but cloud environments change too quickly for periodic snapshots to remain accurate. Automated compliance frameworks, such as

Policy as Code, transform regulatory requirements into executable scripts. These scripts enforce rules consistently across all systems. If a control fails, the system records the event, remediates it, and logs the correction automatically. This creates a verifiable, time-stamped trail of compliance that regulators can review.

The benefits extend beyond regulation. Continuous monitoring improves operational efficiency by reducing human error and freeing experts to focus on strategy rather than repetitive checks. However, automation must never eliminate accountability. Humans remain responsible for setting the rules that machines follow. Ethical oversight ensures that automation enforces fairness, privacy, and proportionality, not just technical accuracy.

The convergence of automation and compliance marks a turning point in financial cybersecurity. It shifts the industry from defending static systems to managing living ecosystems that adapt as fast as the threats they face. In this model, compliance is not a destination but a continuous journey, one that merges technology, ethics, and governance into a single, intelligent rhythm of protection.

CHAPTER NINE

Data Privacy, Ethics, and Regulatory Alignment in Cybersecurity

Data is the currency of the digital economy and nowhere is its value more concentrated than in the financial sector. Every transaction, every account, and every investment produces a stream of data that tells a story about identity, behavior, and trust. Yet, the more valuable data becomes, the greater the responsibility to protect it. In financial cybersecurity, privacy is not only a technical obligation but an ethical and legal imperative. It determines the integrity of institutions and the confidence of the public they serve.

Modern finance depends on the collection and analysis of vast amounts of information. Customer records, credit histories, market analytics, and algorithmic predictions all contribute to operational efficiency. However, every point of collection is also a point of vulnerability. Breaches of financial data can cause more than economic damage; they can destroy reputations and erode the foundation of trust that underpins the financial system. As digital transactions multiply and automation deepens, data privacy has become inseparable from cybersecurity itself.

At the heart of privacy protection lies the principle of **data minimization** — the idea that institutions should collect only what is necessary, store it securely, and retain it only as long as required. Many organizations still operate under the assumption that more data equals more intelligence. In truth, excessive data collection creates unnecessary exposure. By defining clear boundaries around what data is truly essential, institutions not only reduce risk but demonstrate respect for user autonomy. In this sense, privacy becomes a measure of ethical maturity as much as technical competence.

Transparency forms the second pillar of data ethics. Customers have the right to know how their information is being used, who has access to it, and for what purpose. Privacy policies written in dense legal language may satisfy compliance requirements but rarely foster understanding. Clarity, simplicity, and openness transform compliance into communication. When institutions are transparent, they empower customers to make informed decisions about their digital participation. This transparency is not just good ethics; it is good business. Institutions that explain their privacy practices clearly build stronger, more trusting relationships.

In the modern financial ecosystem, compliance frameworks provide the structure within which ethics and technology must coexist. Regulations such as the **General Data Protection Regulation (GDPR)** in Europe, the **California Consumer Privacy Act (CCPA)** in the United States, and Nigeria's **Data Protection Regulation (NDPR)** have redefined global expectations of privacy. These laws establish core principles of consent, accountability, and security. They require institutions to prove that data handling is lawful, transparent, and fair. Non-compliance can result in severe penalties, but more importantly, it can cost the confidence of customers and partners alike.

Regulatory alignment is no longer optional. Financial institutions must integrate compliance into every layer of their operations, from product design to customer service. This integration requires multidisciplinary collaboration. Legal experts interpret obligations, technologists implement controls, and executives ensure alignment with corporate ethics. Together, they create a governance structure that transforms regulation from a constraint into a guiding framework. Continuous compliance monitoring tools now make it possible to track regulatory adherence in real time, replacing periodic audits with dynamic assurance.

The principle of **privacy by design** exemplifies this shift. It requires that privacy protection be built into systems from the beginning rather than added as an afterthought. In financial technology, this means encrypting data at the architectural level, anonymizing analytics, and limiting access from the earliest stages of product development. Privacy by design aligns ethics with innovation, ensuring that progress does not come at the expense of protection. It also encourages collaboration between developers, compliance officers, and customers, who together define what responsible innovation looks like.

Ethics in cybersecurity extends beyond compliance. Laws can mandate behavior, but they cannot guarantee morality. Ethical leadership involves asking not just what is legal but what is right. Financial institutions face complex moral questions: how much surveillance is acceptable to detect fraud, how to balance security with personal freedom, and how to use artificial intelligence responsibly when it processes sensitive financial data. These questions have no simple answers, but they demand continuous reflection. Ethical decision-making must be institutionalized through codes of conduct, internal ethics boards, and transparent accountability mechanisms.

The intersection of ethics and technology is perhaps most visible in the realm of **artificial intelligence and automated decision-making**. AI systems that analyze financial behavior can detect fraud, assess creditworthiness, and personalize investment strategies. Yet, these same systems can also perpetuate bias, discriminate unfairly, or make opaque decisions that affect people's lives. Institutions must therefore ensure **algorithmic transparency** — the ability to explain how AI systems reach their conclusions. Customers should be able to understand why a loan was denied or why a transaction was flagged. Transparency transforms automation from a source of suspicion into a source of trust.

Another dimension of ethical cybersecurity involves **data sharing and collaboration**. Financial institutions increasingly exchange data with regulators, insurers, analytics firms, and cloud providers. While collaboration strengthens security and compliance, it also amplifies privacy risks. Each data exchange introduces new opportunities for misuse. Secure data-sharing frameworks must therefore rely on encryption, contractual obligations, and technical safeguards such as tokenization and secure multiparty computation. The goal is to enable cooperation without compromising confidentiality.

Ethical alignment also means ensuring fairness across global systems. Many developing economies are adopting financial technologies designed elsewhere, often under data regimes less protective than those in advanced markets. Ethical financial institutions must take responsibility for maintaining the same privacy standards regardless of geography. Global operations demand a universal commitment to data dignity — the recognition that every individual, regardless of location, deserves the same respect and protection for their personal information.

In the coming years, **data sovereignty and digital identity** will redefine the balance between privacy and accessibility. Decentralized identity systems will allow users to own and control their credentials, choosing what information to share with institutions. Blockchain and zero-knowledge proof technologies will make it possible to verify authenticity without revealing underlying data. These innovations represent the next step in aligning ethics, privacy, and cybersecurity. They restore agency to individuals and reduce the asymmetry of power between institutions and customers.

Ultimately, data privacy and ethics are not separate from cybersecurity; they are its conscience. A secure system that violates privacy is not truly secure. A compliant system that disregards fairness is not truly ethical. Financial institutions must evolve beyond mere protection toward stewardship, the responsible management of data in the service of trust, transparency, and human dignity. The regulations that govern this evolution are not constraints but compasses, guiding the industry toward a future where innovation and integrity advance together.

9.1 Privacy by Design and Ethical Innovation

The evolution of digital finance has shown that innovation without ethics can be as dangerous as stagnation without progress. Financial institutions once treated privacy as a compliance obligation; something to address after systems were built. Today, the paradigm has shifted toward privacy by design, where protection is integrated into every layer of development. This philosophy redefines how technology is conceived, ensuring that data safety and user dignity are embedded from the very first line of code.

Privacy by design begins with intentionality. Every feature, algorithm, and interface must be evaluated through the lens of data minimization and necessity. Engineers are encouraged to ask critical questions before implementation: What data must we collect? How long should it be retained? Who should have access? Each answer forms part of a transparent privacy framework that aligns innovation with responsibility. Financial institutions that follow this approach build systems where protection is proactive rather than reactive.

Embedding privacy early also simplifies long-term governance. Retroactively fixing privacy flaws in existing systems is costly, both financially and reputationally. By contrast, systems built with ethical foresight are inherently more resilient. This approach reduces vulnerabilities, enhances compliance efficiency, and fosters public trust. When customers sense that an institution values their privacy as much as its own growth, loyalty deepens naturally.

Ethical innovation extends beyond technical safeguards to cultural ones. Development teams must be trained to think ethically about data. Cross-functional collaboration between legal experts, designers, and data scientists ensures that ethical discussions accompany every stage of innovation. Ethics should not slow down progress; it should define its direction. When financial institutions innovate responsibly, they not only protect users but also strengthen the legitimacy of technological advancement itself.

The principle of ethical innovation also demands openness. Institutions that engage the public and regulators transparently in their design processes create accountability. Public consultations, transparency reports, and independent audits transform ethical promises into measurable actions. In the end, privacy by design is not only a framework for compliance but a vision for sustainable progress, one that places human dignity at the center of technological evolution.

9.2 Algorithmic Transparency and Fairness in Finance

Artificial intelligence has become an essential tool in modern financial systems. It detects fraud, assesses risk, recommends investments, and automates regulatory monitoring. Yet, as algorithms gain influence, they also acquire power; power to decide who qualifies for a loan, who is flagged for fraud, or who receives investment opportunities. With such authority comes the urgent need for transparency and fairness.

Algorithmic transparency refers to the ability to understand, explain, and justify how an algorithm reaches its conclusions. In the context of finance, this means being able to trace decisions that affect people's lives and livelihoods. If a customer is denied a mortgage or flagged for suspicious activity, the institution must be able to explain why. Lack of transparency erodes trust, turning technology from a tool of empowerment into one of exclusion. Transparency ensures accountability, allowing both customers and regulators to challenge decisions and verify fairness.

Ensuring fairness in algorithmic systems begins with data. Bias often originates not from malicious intent but from the datasets used to train models. Historical data can reflect social inequalities, which then become mathematically reinforced in automated systems. If past lending favored certain demographics, a machine learning model may inadvertently perpetuate that pattern. Financial institutions must therefore implement **bias detection and correction mechanisms** at every stage of model development. This includes diverse data sampling, independent audits, and fairness testing under multiple demographic conditions.

Regulators worldwide are paying closer attention to these issues. The European Union's proposed **AI Act** and emerging frameworks from the United States, Canada, and Nigeria emphasize explainability and fairness in algorithmic decision-making. These frameworks recognize that financial algorithms, like human employees, must be accountable. Institutions that invest in explainable AI not only meet compliance expectations but also earn customer trust.

Beyond compliance, algorithmic transparency is an ethical obligation. Customers deserve clarity about how their personal information shapes decisions that affect them. Ethical AI design encourages human oversight, ensuring that final accountability remains with people, not machines.

When institutions make algorithms interpretable, they bridge the gap between technical precision and social responsibility.

The pursuit of fairness also strengthens resilience. Transparent systems are easier to audit, adjust, and defend. When an algorithm's reasoning can be explained, errors can be corrected without undermining confidence. This adaptability transforms transparency from a regulatory checkbox into a competitive advantage. Institutions that treat algorithmic fairness as a strategic priority position themselves at the forefront of ethical financial innovation.

Algorithmic transparency and fairness remind the industry that technology, however advanced, must remain subordinate to ethics. In a world increasingly governed by data, fairness is the currency of credibility. Financial institutions that balance intelligence with integrity will not only comply with laws but also embody the moral leadership that the digital age demands.

CHAPTER TEN

The Future of Financial Cybersecurity, Innovation, Governance, and Global Resilience

The future of financial cybersecurity will not be written by chance. It will be shaped by the decisions made today; decisions about how institutions innovate, how they govern technology, and how they prepare for the unknown. The digital financial system has evolved from isolated databases to borderless ecosystems powered by artificial intelligence, blockchain, quantum computing, and cloud infrastructure. These technologies have multiplied both opportunity and risk. What emerges from this convergence is a landscape defined by complexity, speed, and interdependence. To survive and thrive within it, financial institutions must think beyond protection and focus on resilience, governance, and global cooperation.

The financial world is now inseparable from the digital one. Transactions once recorded in ledgers are now executed in milliseconds across decentralized networks. This transformation has democratized access to finance but has also introduced vulnerabilities that transcend national boundaries. Cyber threats no longer target single organizations; they exploit interconnected infrastructures. A disruption in one region can ripple through global markets in minutes. As systems grow more intelligent, so do the adversaries who challenge them. The future will demand a kind of security that learns, adapts, and anticipates, a security that sees itself not as a barrier but as an enabler of trust.

Innovation will be the first defining factor of this future. Artificial intelligence will play an increasingly central role in predictive defense, enabling systems to identify emerging threats before they materialize. Advanced behavioral analytics will detect anomalies invisible to the human eye, allowing financial institutions to act before breaches occur. However, innovation in cybersecurity cannot exist in isolation from ethical reasoning. As technologies evolve, so must the moral frameworks that guide their use. Financial institutions must ensure that innovation serves humanity, not the other way around.

Governance will be the second pillar of future resilience. Cybersecurity is no longer the domain of IT departments alone; it is a strategic concern that reaches boardrooms and policy chambers. Institutions will need governance models that integrate risk management, compliance, and ethics under a unified vision. Boards of directors will be expected to understand cyber risks as deeply as they understand balance sheets. Regulators, in turn, will shift from enforcing compliance to fostering collaboration. The governance of the future will be adaptive; informed by data, driven by transparency, and grounded in accountability.

Global resilience will be the third and perhaps most crucial dimension. The threats of tomorrow will not respect borders, and neither should defense. International cooperation among governments, financial regulators, and private institutions will determine the stability of the global financial system. Information sharing, cross-border response protocols, and harmonized regulations will form the foundation of collective protection. Just as the global economy relies on interconnected trade, so must it rely on interconnected security. Institutions that view cybersecurity as a shared responsibility rather than a competitive advantage will set the standard for sustainable resilience.

The convergence of finance and technology also calls for new kinds of partnerships. Collaboration between fintech innovators and traditional banks will drive progress in security solutions. Research institutions will play a larger role in developing quantum-resistant cryptography, decentralized identity systems, and autonomous defense networks. These partnerships will require openness and trust; qualities not traditionally associated with competitive industries. Yet, in cybersecurity, cooperation is not a weakness but a survival strategy.

The future will also bring new regulatory paradigms. Traditional compliance models, which rely on periodic audits and static controls, will be replaced by **real-time regulatory monitoring**. Regulators will gain access to anonymized transaction data streams that allow them to observe systemic risks as they develop. Financial institutions will need to implement infrastructures that can communicate directly with oversight systems through secure, automated interfaces. This shift will redefine accountability from a retrospective obligation into an ongoing relationship between regulators and institutions.

A growing focus on **digital ethics** will further shape how cybersecurity evolves. The rise of surveillance technologies, automated decision-making, and predictive algorithms raises questions about privacy and autonomy. The financial systems of the future must ensure that efficiency does not come at the cost of freedom. Ethical cybersecurity will require not only technical precision but moral clarity. Decisions about data collection, surveillance limits, and user consent must be made through transparent, inclusive processes. The institutions that uphold these values will command the greatest trust in an age of digital scrutiny.

At the technological frontier, the combination of quantum computing and artificial intelligence will redefine the possibilities of both attack and defense. Quantum computing will challenge existing cryptographic systems, but it will also enable unprecedented levels of data processing for fraud detection, transaction validation, and systemic risk modeling. Artificial intelligence, when guided responsibly, will make cybersecurity more adaptive, autonomous, and predictive. The key will be balance, ensuring that the same technologies used to protect systems are not misused to manipulate or control.

Resilience in the future will also depend on people. No matter how advanced technology becomes, it will remain guided by human intent. Cybersecurity leaders must cultivate cultures that value learning, adaptability, and ethical decision-making. Continuous education will become essential as new threats and tools emerge. The professionals who succeed will be those who combine technical skill with emotional intelligence, capable of leading teams through crises with calm and foresight. In the end, resilience is as much a human quality as it is a technical one.

Global financial cybersecurity will also require **inclusivity**. Emerging markets, often the most vulnerable to digital threats, must be integrated into global defense strategies. Cybersecurity capacity building, through training, investment, and infrastructure support will prevent the creation of digital hierarchies where only the wealthiest nations are protected. The stability of the financial world depends on the security of all its participants. Inclusion is therefore not charity; it is strategy.

The future of financial cybersecurity will not be defined solely by technology but by the principles guiding its use. Transparency, fairness, accountability, and empathy will be as essential as encryption and automation. The institutions that lead this future will not only defend assets but also safeguard the values that sustain trust in the financial system. They will understand that cybersecurity is not a product but a philosophy, a way of thinking about protection, power, and responsibility in a connected world.

10.1 Global Collaboration and the Ethics of Innovation

The evolution of global finance has blurred the lines between nations, institutions, and technologies. Money now flows faster than legislation, and data travels farther than jurisdiction. This interconnectedness means that no single country or corporation can secure itself in isolation. Cybersecurity in finance has become a collective responsibility, and the future will depend on how effectively the world can collaborate to protect shared digital assets.

True global collaboration begins with trust. Governments, regulators, and private institutions must share intelligence, align regulations, and develop standards that transcend borders. Initiatives such as international threat intelligence exchanges, regional cybersecurity centers, and global resilience frameworks are early steps in this direction. However, collaboration must extend beyond technical coordination. It must also include the ethical dimension of innovation — an understanding that every technological advancement carries social and moral consequences.

The ethics of innovation call for responsibility at every stage of progress. As artificial intelligence, quantum computing, and blockchain reshape finance, leaders must ensure that these tools are developed with fairness and inclusivity in mind. Ethical innovation promotes transparency, respects privacy, and seeks to balance economic growth with social stability. It discourages digital colonialism, where powerful institutions impose technologies on less developed markets without adequate protection or consent. Instead, it fosters a global culture of shared progress, where technological advancements benefit all participants in the financial ecosystem.

International governance structures will be critical to maintaining this balance. Future cooperation may include global cybersecurity treaties, cross-border regulatory harmonization, and ethical guidelines enforced by multinational councils. These frameworks can prevent jurisdictional gaps that criminals exploit and promote mutual accountability among states and institutions. The future of secure finance depends on the willingness of global actors to see cybersecurity not as a matter of competition but as a universal public good.

Ethical innovation also requires that institutions uphold transparency about how emerging technologies are used. Artificial intelligence systems that monitor transactions or assess risk must be auditable. Quantum computing applications in finance must respect principles of fairness and equality. The power to innovate must be tempered by the wisdom to do so responsibly. The world's financial stability will depend not just on how fast institutions can innovate, but on how wisely they can cooperate.

10.2 Human-Centered Resilience and the Next Frontier

As the financial world races toward automation, one truth remains constant: technology cannot secure what humanity does not value. The future of financial cybersecurity will rely on more than algorithms and encryption; it will depend on the preservation of human judgment, compassion, and adaptability. The next frontier of security is not purely technical but human-centered.

Human-centered resilience recognizes that every security system ultimately serves people. The confidence of customers, the skill of cybersecurity professionals, and the integrity of leadership together determine whether systems endure crises or collapse under them. This perspective places empathy and communication alongside coding and analytics as essential tools of cybersecurity. In moments of disruption, what sustains trust is not only how quickly systems recover but how authentically institutions communicate.

The integration of human understanding into digital systems will shape the next wave of innovation. Cybersecurity tools of the future will not only detect threats but interpret intent. Interfaces will become more intuitive, designed to reduce human error rather than punish it. Artificial intelligence will assist professionals by filtering noise and amplifying meaningful insights, allowing them to focus on judgment and strategy. The partnership between human intuition and machine intelligence will become the cornerstone of adaptive resilience.

The education of the next generation of cybersecurity professionals will also evolve. Beyond technical mastery, they will need to understand ethics, psychology, and global policy. The defenders of tomorrow must be thinkers as well as technicians, capable of bridging the divide between systems and societies. Universities, professional organizations, and financial institutions must therefore reimagine their training programs to produce leaders who can defend not just infrastructure but integrity.

The final measure of resilience will be inclusivity. The cybersecurity ecosystem of the future must ensure that every region, regardless of its level of development, has access to knowledge, tools, and protection. Capacity building in developing economies will help close the security divide that currently separates advanced markets from emerging ones. Shared training programs, international funding, and open-access resources can create a truly global defense network. In this shared future, security becomes a language that unites rather than divides.

Human-centered resilience completes the circle of progress. It reminds the industry that the ultimate goal of cybersecurity is not to build perfect systems, but to build enduring confidence. The financial institutions that combine technology with empathy, innovation with ethics, and intelligence with humility will lead the world into a future where security becomes synonymous with trust. The frontier ahead is vast, but it is navigable, if guided by the timeless principles of integrity, collaboration, and respect for human dignity.

REVIEWS

1. Dr. Chijioke Nwogu – Chief Information Security Officer, Access Bank Plc

This book captures the essence of cybersecurity in finance with both intelligence and clarity. Tolulope Komolafe brings a deep awareness of how technology, risk, and human behavior intersect the financial ecosystem. Her explanations of compliance-driven frameworks such as GDPR and PCI DSS show not only technical depth but strategic foresight. I found her approach to multi-layered fraud detection particularly relevant to the challenges we face in large financial institutions.

2. Prof. Hauwa Ibrahim – Dean, Faculty of Computing and Information Technology, Ahmadu Bello University

As an academic who has studied cybersecurity for over two decades, I find Tolulope's work refreshing for its balance of theory and practicality. She moves effortlessly between global trends and local realities, showing how financial systems in emerging economies can adopt global standards without losing contextual relevance. The sections on artificial intelligence, blockchain, and secure cloud systems are both rigorous and accessible.

3. Adebayo Adesina – Founder, Fin Secure Technologies

For those of us building solutions at the frontier of financial technology, this book provides a much-needed blueprint for sustainability. Many fintech startups focus on speed, scalability, and user experience while neglecting the structural foundations of security. Tolulope Komolafe reminds us that innovation without protection is instability disguised as progress.

4. Dr. Ozioma Umeh – Director, Cybersecurity Policy and Standards, Central Bank of Nigeria

From a policy perspective, Tolulope's book is both a revelation and a roadmap. It offers a thoughtful synthesis of how cybersecurity measures can align with regulatory intent while still encouraging innovation. Her advocacy for stronger collaboration between financial regulators, technology developers, and data protection agencies is both timely and persuasive. I was particularly impressed by her treatment of compliance as a living framework rather than a static obligation.

5. Chinenye Okafor – Lead Cyber Risk Consultant, Deloitte Nigeria

Tolulope Komolafe writes with the precision of a cybersecurity professional and the empathy of someone who understands how failures affect people, not just systems. Her approach to risk management is holistic, combining technology, governance, and awareness into one unified vision. The section on secure auditing platforms and threat intelligence stood out for its practical relevance. What makes this book exceptional is that it does not stop at diagnosis; it provides actionable frameworks for building resilience.

REFERENCES

Al-Ruithe, M., Benkhelifa, E., & Hameed, K. (2019). Data governance taxonomy: Cloud versus non-cloud. *Journal of Cloud Computing*, 8(1), 1–22. https://doi.org/10.1186/s13677-018-0123-7

Arner, D. W., Barberis, J., & Buckley, R. P. (2016). The evolution of Fintech: A new post-crisis paradigm? *Georgetown Journal of International Law*, 47(4), 1271–1319.

Basel Committee on Banking Supervision. (2021). *Principles for operational resilience.* Bank for International Settlements. https://www.bis.org/bcbs/publ/d516.pdf

Bélanger, F., & Crossler, R. E. (2011). Privacy in the digital age: A review of information privacy research in information systems. *MIS Quarterly*, 35(4), 1017–1041. https://doi.org/10.2307/41409971

Brennen, S., & Kreiss, D. (2016). Digitalization. In *The International Encyclopedia of Communication Theory and Philosophy* (pp. 1–11). Wiley-Blackwell. https://doi.org/10.1002/9781118766804.wbiect111

European Union Agency for Cybersecurity. (2023). *Threat landscape report 2023: Emerging trends in cybersecurity*. ENISA. https://www.enisa.europa.eu

Gai, K., Qiu, M., & Sun, X. (2018). A survey on FinTech. *Journal of Network and Computer Applications*, 103, 262–273. https://doi.org/10.1016/j.jnca.2017.10.011

Kshetri, N. (2021). *Cybersecurity and business: Strategies for protecting your business from cybercrime*. Springer Nature. https://doi.org/10.1007/978-3-030-66051-9

Mouzas, S. (2022). Cybersecurity in financial services: Managing trust and resilience. *Journal of Business Research*, 139, 873–882. https://doi.org/10.1016/j.jbusres.2021.10.065

National Institute of Standards and Technology. (2020). *Framework for improving critical infrastructure cybersecurity* (Version 1.1). U.S. Department of Commerce. https://doi.org/10.6028/NIST.CSWP.04162018

Pahl, C., Jamshidi, P., & Weyns, D. (2019). Cloud resilience: Concepts, frameworks, and challenges. *IEEE Software*, 36(3), 78–85. https://doi.org/10.1109/MS.2018.290111010

Reinsel, D., Gantz, J., & Rydning, J. (2018). *The digitalization of the world from edge to core*. IDC White Paper, Seagate Technology.

Solove, D. J., & Schwartz, P. M. (2021). *Information privacy law* (7th ed.). Wolters Kluwer.

Stulz, R. M. (2019). FinTech, bigtech, and the future of banks. *Journal of Applied Corporate Finance*, 31(4), 86–97. https://doi.org/10.1111/jacf.12388

Taddeo, M., & Floridi, L. (2018). How AI can be a force for good. *Science*, 361(6404), 751–752. https://doi.org/10.1126/science.aat5991

World Economic Forum. (2022). *Global cybersecurity outlook 2022*. World Economic Forum. https://www.weforum.org/reports/global-cybersecurity-outlook-2022

Zhou, W., Arner, D. W., & Buckley, R. P. (2015). Regulating FinTech innovation: A balancing act. *Hong Kong Law Journal*, 45(2), 369–418.

www.ingramcontent.com/pod-product-compliance
Lightning Source LLC
La Vergne TN
LVHW101503200926
848483LV00001B/216